THE
SECRET
LIFE OF
JOHN
LE CARRÉ

SECRET LIFE OF JOHN LE CARRÉ

ADAM SISMAN

HARPER

An Imprint of HarperCollins*Publishers*

HarperCollins books may be purchased for educational, business, or sales promotional use. For information, please email the Special Markets Department at SPsales@harpercollins.com.

Originally published in Great Britain in 2023 by Profile Books.

FIRST U.S. EDITION

Library of Congress Cataloging-in-Publication Data has been applied for.

ISBN 978-0-06-334104-3

23 24 25 26 27 LBC 5 4 3 2 1

'All his life he's been inventing versions
of himself that are untrue'

A Perfect Spy

Contents

THE SECRET LIFE OF JOHN LE CARRÉ

Introduction: candour & guile

Why write the 'secret life' of John le Carré? Is it right to make public aspects of his existence that he strove so hard to keep private? In writing this book I was conscious that some might consider the subject matter prurient. And to some extent I accept this criticism; if it were no more than an exposé of adultery, then reading it would be not much better than voyeurism. In her book *The Silent Woman: Sylvia Plath and Ted Hughes* (1994), Janet Malcolm pilloried the professional biographer as a voyeur and a busybody, colluding with the reader 'in an excitingly forbidden undertaking: tiptoeing down the corridor together, to stand in front of the bedroom door and try to peep through the keyhole'. That has not been my usual practice. Rather than peeping through the keyhole, I have tended to linger in the corridor, clearing my throat to indicate my presence. I am not one of those that believes that sex explains everything. On the contrary, it seems to me that for most people sex is merely part of ordinary life, not the creative spark.

But in the case of John le Carré, whose real name was David Cornwell, his pursuit of women was a key to unlock his fiction. Not only did it help to explain what he wrote, it helped to explain how, why and when he wrote. David himself was explicit on this point. 'My infidelities,' he wrote to me at a time when, for better or worse, the issue had come to dominate our discussions,

> produced in my life a duality & a tension that became almost a necessary drug for my writing, a dangerous edge of some kind … They are not therefore a 'dark part' of my life, separate from the 'high literary calling', so to speak, but, alas, integral to it, & inseparable.

Nonetheless he restricted what I was able to write about his affairs in his lifetime, as I detail in the last chapter of this book. My biography of John le Carré, published in 2015, was the truth, insofar as I was able to ascertain it, but not the whole truth. While David was alive, I was obliged to suppress some of what I knew.

Eight years on, there is no remaining reason for reticence. 'I don't care what you write about me after I'm dead,' David said to me on several occasions. He died towards the end of 2020, at the age of eighty-nine, after sustaining a fall in his bathroom, and his wife Jane died only weeks later, after a long struggle with cancer. As for the rest of his family, his three surviving sons feel that, in general, any information about their father that may aid understanding of his work should be on the public record. Now that he is dead, we can know him better.

Besides, the cat is out of the bag. In October 2022 one of his lovers, using the pseudonym Suleika Dawson, published a memoir of their time together. A few weeks later, a volume of le Carré letters appeared, edited by his son Tim (who tragically died while the book was in press); this included two letters from Susan Anderson, another woman with whom David had an affair. These letters are part of a larger collection, available for scrutiny in a public archive. The story of David's involvement with these two women is recounted in the pages of this book, together with the stories of other women with whom he was involved at one time or another. Cumulatively they provide a picture of a man always restlessly seeking love, for whom extra-marital affairs were not a distraction from his writing, but an essential stimulus.

*

'It's hard not to feel that there is a great deal we're not being told,' wrote Theo Tait, in a review of my biography for the *London Review of Books*. He was right, of course. In his review, Tait differentiated between the first half of the book, which, he wrote, does 'exactly what you want a biography of a novelist to do'; and the second half, which he found much less revealing. 'At a certain point the reader is banished from Cornwell's life.' That point was the moment David met Jane, who became his second wife in 1972. As Tait observed, she took on the role of gatekeeper; and from then on the gate was kept tightly shut.

Tait was one of several reviewers to perceive that the book was the outcome of a struggle between author and subject: 'a truce between candour and guile', as Robert McCrum put it in the *Observer*. My book benefited from access to my subject and his archive, but this came at a cost. In theory I was free to write what I thought fit; but in practice I was constrained. There was the obvious factor that it would have been difficult to proceed had le Carré withdrawn his co-operation, as seemed possible at one stage. Given that he was so protective of his privacy, I found myself questioning why David had agreed to co-operate with me, after seeing off several suitors in the past. Inasmuch as I was able to answer the question, I came to believe that he had two, partly contradictory motives: he wanted a serious biography commensurate with his stature as a serious writer, and he wanted to be able to control what was in it. One seasoned le Carré watcher believes that he encouraged the biography because he hoped to find out about himself, only to recoil in dismay when I held up the mirror.

Undertaking a life of a living person is always a compromise. Even an unauthorised biographer is inhibited by the law of libel. As biographers of T. S. Eliot and Ted Hughes have discovered to their cost, the law of copyright is another inhibitor when writing about a writer, because (broadly speaking) the writings of the living (or recently dead) may not be quoted without permission. The position is more ambiguous when a biography is being written with the consent of the subject; or even more so when the subject co-operates with the biographer. In a previous book I explored the tension between the two. The subject is, almost by definition, the senior figure; the biographer is in a subordinate position. Each is thinking about posterity. In any agreement between them there will be an element of *quid pro quo*: while the subject remains alive he or she retains some measure of control, even if the restraints are rarely visible. But the biographer is likely to have the last word.

Of course it is helpful to the biographer to meet and to become familiar with his or her subject (though not so helpful as one might imagine), but the more you come to know someone, the less inclined you are to upset them. Familiarity with your subject can be both an advantage and a handicap.

The recent history of biography offers contrasting precedents.

James Atlas's memoir *The Shadow in the Garden: A Biographer's Tale* (2017) recounts in excruciating detail the succession of mishaps and mistakes he made in writing his life of Saul Bellow, like mine published while his subject was still alive, in 2000. On the other hand, Patrick French was able to publish *The World Is What It Is* (2008), his authorised biography of V. S. Naipaul, during his subject's lifetime, despite the fact that his book revealed damaging details about Naipaul's private behaviour. 'A great writer requires a great biography,' George Packer wrote in his *New York Times* review of French's book, 'and a great biography must tell the truth.'

I had been aware from the outset that dealing with David wasn't going to be easy. Robert Harris, who had been commissioned to write a life of le Carré almost twenty years earlier, warned me that I would never be able to publish in his lifetime. As it turned out he was wrong, but only partially so.

At the start David was welcoming, and we were immediately on first-name terms, so friendly that I often had to remind myself that we weren't really friends at all, and that the cordiality could be withdrawn at any time – as I found had happened to others who thought of themselves as his friends.

Perhaps it helped that I was, and remain, an admirer of his work. In my opinion he is a writer of high class, worthy of comparison with the best. Assuming that people are still reading novels in a hundred years' time, I think there is a good chance that they will be reading le Carré. For me, he is the definitive writer of the Cold War era: more than that, he is (as Blake Morrison has put it) 'a laureate' of Britain's 'post-imperial sleepwalk' – a sleep from which, arguably, we have yet to wake. Like most readers, I think more highly of some of his books than others, and like many I think less well of the later novels than the ones written in what I consider to be his prime, from the mid-1960s to the mid-1980s. Naturally David wanted one to admire all his work, his most recent most of all.

In the introduction to my biography I described an episode that occurred early on. I had driven down to Cornwall for my first visit to Tregiffian, his isolated house on the cliffs above the shoreline near Land's End, where his papers were kept. To reach it you had to turn off the road and drive several hundred yards along a grassy track towards the sea. I had not yet seen David when Jane set me to work, in an outhouse that served as his archive. It was a beautiful spring morning, so sunny and warm that I left the door ajar. After I had been there an hour or so I became aware of a shadow, and looked up from my desk to see David standing over my shoulder. It's an image that stays in the reader's mind, according to Tait:

> The book depicts Cornwell as a man you wouldn't want to cross: very clever and very touchy; helpful and generous towards those he trusts, but unforgiving and vindictive towards those he sees as a threat or a disappointment.

The crisis in my relations with David came after I began to uncover evidence of his extramarital affairs. In doing so I cannot claim any special skills as a detective; on the contrary, I learned about his lovers almost at random. I was told about one by some fellow guests at lunch with friends one Sunday; I heard about another late at night at a party, from someone I had just met. David's half-sister Charlotte told me about another lover, an American photographer. When I contacted her, she responded openly, offering to talk; but after she had been in touch with

David, her attitude changed completely. 'I want no part in your book,' she wrote to me. I heard about yet another woman, an Italian journalist, from a writer who knew David well. To him, she had spoken freely about her affair with David; but to me, she pretended that it had been a misunderstanding. As soon as one of David's ex-lovers opened her mouth, it seemed, David shut her up.

I was not especially interested in David's private life *per se*, though I could scarcely ignore the fact that betrayal was a recurrent theme of his work. It did occur to me too that a man who lives a double life is a man under constant pressure. Did this pressure energise the work? The life of a writer, even a bestselling writer, is not in itself very exciting: in essence it involves sitting alone in a room, with pen or keyboard. Tait was not the only reviewer to comment that the most interesting part of the biography was the story of my subject's early years, before David Cornwell became John le Carré, and a few years afterwards. Perhaps the drama of the later years was hidden. Were sexual adventures a relief from the tedium of the writing life? Was the excitement of adultery, with the risk of exposure, a stimulus to creativity? Was it a substitute for spying?

*

John le Carré was an enigma, which made him a tempting subject for a biographer. From the beginning of his career as a writer in the early 1960s there had been speculation about him: in particular, about the extent to which his novels drew on his own experience. Almost inevitably his readers become intrigued by the writer. Even his pseudonym was a mystery. He provided several different explanations of why he chose the name John le Carré, and afterwards admitted that none of these was true.

Few were convinced by his early denials that he had been a spy. Later he admitted to having served in British intelligence; but the more he protested that this had been merely in a humble capacity, the more suspicion spread that he had really been a spymaster. Such ambiguity served his purpose. One feature of his intelligence background is that it allowed his often-cryptic utterances to go unchallenged, because they seemed based on secret knowledge. One can see why it was sometimes necessary for him to obfuscate, but at other times this seemed to arise from no more than a cultivated air of mystery. He encouraged the sense that he was concealing more than he revealed. And his long-lasting success meant that he was interviewed time after time, decade after decade. Each interviewer would mug up beforehand on what he had said in the past and push him to say more. The inevitable result was that his autobiography became more colourful as time passed. Hints hardened into facts, and tall stories became taller.

In a piece he wrote after my book was published David would regret having given so many interviews, which he conceded was 'not a process that is compatible with self-knowledge'. He summed it up as follows: 'First you invent yourself, then you get to believe your invention.'

One example of this is the writing of his breakthrough novel, *The Spy Who Came in from the Cold*. The book was a great leap forward from the two novels he had written before, and it seems plausible that he wrote it in a burst of creative energy, as he often suggested. But, in his telling, that outpouring of creative energy became more and more compressed as the years passed.

In a television interview given almost forty years after the book was published, for example, he claimed that he had written the book in a mere five weeks, in an anguished response to the Berlin Wall going up. In fact the border between East and West Berlin had been sealed, and construction of the Berlin Wall had started, a full fifteen months before the manuscript of the book was submitted to his publishers. He actually wrote the book in eight months: still impressively quick for such a complex book.

Everything he said, therefore, needed to be examined sceptically. David often spoke about his refusal to meet 'Kim' Philby,* the most notorious and perhaps the most successful of Soviet double agents, when the opportunity arose on a visit to Moscow in 1987. By 2010, when he gave an interview to Olga Craig of the *Telegraph*, this decision had become elevated to one of the highest principle. 'I couldn't possibly have shook his hand,' he told her. 'It was drenched in blood. It would have been repulsive.' But the diary of his travelling companion records David as saying at the time that he would 'dearly love' to meet Philby one day – 'purely for zoological purposes, of course!'

This was not necessarily a paradox. Confronted with the opportunity to meet Philby, David recoiled from an encounter that he had been willing to contemplate in principle. Such discrepancies, if indeed they are discrepancies, are not, in my opinion, examples of bad faith, but merely evidence that David, like all of us, edited his past as he revisited it, which he did more than most people. He reimagined incidents in his past for his

---

* His real name was Harold, but from his schooldays on he was always known as Kim, after the eponymous boy-spy hero of Kipling's novel. Like Kim, Philby had been born in India.

John le Carré   9 Gainsborough gdns
NW3 1BJ

15 July 2010

Dear Mr Sisman,

Let me say first that I was on the point of going up to Waterstone's in Hampstead to buy your book on H T-R when your letter arrived: so thank you for it, and for what you kindly say about my work. I am, as you may suppose, very divided about how to respond — flattered by your interest, + consoled by it, since I have had similar letters from biographers whom I do not rate highly — and I think, as you say,

David Cornwell's first letter to me, 15 July 2010.

2

John le Carré

it would be best to meet, + explore the possibilities. There are huge hindrances: my own messy private life, the demise of so many people I worked with or otherwise knew, and my habitual reluctance to discuss my very limited + unspectacular career in intelligence. I see you finding disenchantment everywhere, + your readers doing the same, and I worry, of course, about my children + grandchildren, probably quite unnecessarily. Anyway, do let's meet & talk, if only

John le Carré

3

that I may give you the longer version of my relationships with HT-R, from which I emerge an even bigger fool than the one he describes.

I haven't read your 'Hugh' from beginning to end, just dipped, but let me in passing congratulate you on its splendid reception, & thank you again for writing. Like HT-R, I would wish you to write without restraints: perhaps that's the problem!

With best wishes,

David Cornwell

fiction, and what he remembered afterwards tended to be the fictional reimagining rather than what had actually occurred.

*

The appearance of my biography in 2015 dispelled some of the myths about David's past. It was based on an agreement we had reached at the outset. He did not want me to use the term 'authorised', presumably so that he could distance himself from what I wrote if he so chose, but we agreed that my book should be definitive, insofar as this was possible. I have little doubt that one of his motives for encouraging me was *pour décourager les autres*.

My involvement with David Cornwell started in the most straightforward fashion. I wrote him a letter, proposing myself as his biographer, and he responded, inviting me to come and see him at his house in Hampstead to discuss the suggestion. This was in the summer of 2010. My timing was opportune, as I would discover: he was just beginning to read my most recent book, a biography of the historian Hugh Trevor-Roper. David had known Trevor-Roper slightly and had clashed with him on two separate occasions, almost twenty years apart. When we met a week or so later, he told me that he had enjoyed my portrayal of Trevor-Roper's combative personality.

He made it clear from the beginning that he wished me to write 'without restraints', which was what I wanted too. I estimated that it would take me four years to write, as proved to be the case. We came to an agreement, by which David (as he quickly became to me) granted me access to his archives, a list of introductions to people he had known (friends and enemies) and an indefinite number of extended interviews.

In his reply to my initial letter David had highlighted two biographical problems: one was 'my habitual reluctance to discuss my very limited & unspectacular career in intelligence', and the other was what he called 'my own messy private life'. I was able to overcome the first problem, at least to my own satisfaction. Though David remained silent about his intelligence work, I heard about it nonetheless. If I could not provide all the details, I was able to show how, when and where he worked throughout. I was able to trace his career in espionage, from his recruitment by MI6 in post-war Berne while still a teenager, as a source of low-level intelligence and as an occasional 'mule'; his National Service in the Intelligence Corps in occupied Austria; his re-recruitment as an informer by MI5, while an undergraduate at Oxford, when he befriended left-wing students in order to spy on them; his service with MI5 in his mid-twenties, vetting candidates for senior positions who might prove a security risk, and running agents in the Communist Party; and finally his transfer to MI6 and his service in what was then West Germany, working out of the British Embassy in Bonn. There he wrote *The Spy Who Came in from the Cold*, a colossal bestseller, on a scale that happens perhaps only once in a decade. It reached the top of the bestseller list on both sides of the Atlantic, and remained there for week after week, far outselling one of Ian Fleming's James Bond books published around the same time, *On Her Majesty's Secret Service*. Its enormous success enabled David to retire from spying to concentrate on writing; after the age of thirty-three he would never hold another job of any kind.

*

His marriage to Jane was often characterised in public as an ideal partnership. 'I think we're more monogamous than most couples,' he told one visitor. It's hard to know what he meant by this if it wasn't meant ironically, because the truth is that he was serially unfaithful. Without much effort I was able to identify eleven women with whom he had affairs during the first thirty years of their marriage, and I am aware that there were plenty more besides these. Of the eleven, three are now dead (one was killed in a road accident, one by a terrorist bomb, and one took her own life, years after her affair with David had ended), and two repelled my approaches – but the remaining six have talked to me, at length. In recounting their stories I have been conscious that what he told them may not always have been true, though confided in private. Sometimes what he told one woman cannot be reconciled with what he told another. We may not be able to judge to whom he was lying; all we can say for certain is that he was lying to somebody.

Several of these women are recognisable as characters in his novels. Lizzie Worthington in *The Honourable Schoolboy* is based on one of them; Tessa Quayle in *The Constant Gardener* on another. Most of them were younger than he was, some of them much younger. One was the au pair looking after his youngest son. With another woman, almost thirty years his junior, he had two affairs: the first in the mid-1980s, the second fourteen years later. His last that I know about was with a journalist more than forty years younger. Though married with young children by the time I spoke to her, she told me that she considered the relationship with David the most important in her life.

When David decided to seduce a woman, he would pursue her relentlessly, using the manifold gifts at his disposal. A handsome man even in late middle age, he could be scintillating company, witty and attentive, with a fund of entertaining stories and a deep reservoir of experience to draw upon. He wrote playful and erotic letters to his lovers, making them feel missed and desired. He lured those with literary ambitions into imagining that they might write together. Like his father, he had the ability to make people love him even when they knew that they shouldn't, and to want to protect him and share his life. And he had deep pockets, so that he was able to take women to the finest hotels and restaurants, drape them with jewellery, pay their rent, and fly them overseas for erotic assignations.

Why did David pursue these women with such intensity, and what does it say about him? When compelled to confront this issue, he told me that the restless, self-destructive search for love was part of his nature. In his mind this went back to his childhood, to his unrequited love for his mother, who abandoned her children at an early age. Perhaps too he was influenced by German literature, particularly the literature of early German romanticism, which took a grip on him at an early age and remained close to his heart, encouraging a tendency towards heighted emotion and self-dramatisation. Several of his novels culminate in the protagonist's suicide – which, he told his long-term editor Roland Philipps, was the ultimate romantic conclusion. The founding text of the German Romantic movement is Goethe's *The Sorrows of Young Werther*, which reaches its culmination when Werther, despairing of unrequited love, shoots himself with a pistol given to him by his beloved.

David claimed that these extramarital relationships were 'impulsive, driven, short-lived affairs ... often meaningless in themselves', but while that might be true of some of them, others appear to have been much more serious and long-lasting.

He needed to be loved, and at times seems to have believed himself to have been in love, at least in the moment. He told several women that he was willing to leave his wife for them. Of course he did not do so. Whether this was a tactic, or whether he meant it at the time, is an open question. Perhaps he was not really capable of love. 'That's what I do,' he has Barley Blair, protagonist of *The Russia House* (1989), say. 'I bewitch people, then the moment they're under my spell I cease to feel anything for them.' Much the same is true of his *alter ego* Magnus Pym, in his autobiographical novel *A Perfect Spy* (1986). 'He's the Pym who can't rest till he's touched the love in people,' Pym himself admits to his confessor, Jack Brotherhood, 'then can't rest till he's hacked his way out of it.'

'I must go and lie to my wife,' he told one lover, as he rose from the hotel bed and padded towards the telephone. Though he took great care to hide what he was up to from Jane, she inevitably became aware of some of it, and it was hard for her, especially as she had to suffer David's infidelities in silence most of the time. Occasionally her misery would erupt: just before his sixtieth birthday, for example. 'You don't have to celebrate with me, if there's someone else,' she burst out, in front of an embarrassed visitor. He proposed to one, a particularly glamorous woman (a former model), that she should move in with them, to form a *ménage à trois*. Jane told herself that 'nobody can have all of David'. He flattered her that her input was important to his work, but he said the same to other women too. Each in turn became his 'muse'. His writing pal James Kennaway advised David that he would need a different woman for each book, advice David appears to have taken to heart. Thus Liese Deniz inspired *The Honourable Schoolboy*, Verity Mosley and Janet Lee

Stevens *The Little Drummer Girl*, Sue Dawson *A Perfect Spy*, the Italian journalist *The Russia House*, Susan Anderson *The Tailor of Panama* and to some extent *Our Game* also, Yvette Pierpaoli *The Constant Gardener*, and so on.

David's adulterous behaviour during his second marriage followed a precedent established in his first. When he read the first draft of my biography, he grumbled that I had given too much importance to his involvement with Susie and James Kennaway in the mid-1960s, 'in relation to greater and more formative influences later on'. I could scarcely avoid the subject, as all three had published books about the affair, David's being his only non-espionage novel, the disastrous *The Naïve and Sentimental Lover* (1971). This was another *ménage à trois*, in which the emotions ran high between all three. One evening the trio went together to the cinema to see *Jules et Jim*, and Susie sat in the dark between the two men, holding hands with both. David wanted me to remove some of the details, particularly his 'toe-curlingly' impassioned letters to James Kennaway, whom he addressed as 'dearest James' and 'lovely boy'. And he insisted too that I remove any mention of his affair in the mid-1960s with his secretary Liz Tollinton, on grounds that seemed to me spurious: that this might upset his sons.

This subject of his adultery was one which loomed large over the writing of my biography. As I progressed, and inevitably uncovered more discomfiting details, David became agitated, and wrote to me in increasingly fervent terms. Our relations became strained. The book was able to proceed only after mediation by his eldest son, Simon, who visited me in Bristol to discuss the project. He fully agreed with me that David's relations with women were key to a full understanding of his work, and proposed that I should keep 'a secret annexe' for eventual publication in some form after both David and Jane were dead. The secret annexe is the basis of this book. It is not a substitute for or a condensation of my 2015 biography, but a supplement, containing material that I felt obliged to omit then, as well as information that has emerged since. It might be described as What Was Left Out. To make this book comprehensible to readers who might not have read the biography I have included a few paragraphs from the latter, but otherwise there is no overlap between the two.

'I am a writer who was a spy, not a spy who writes novels,' David told his friend Federico Varese, an academic specialising in studies of the Russian mafia. John le Carré was a major writer, but David Cornwell was only a very minor spy. He always hid behind his security cover, maintaining that he could not talk about his comparatively unimportant intelligence work. This made it difficult for me to deal with the subject; he could always trump anything that I wrote by suggesting that there was more that he was regrettably unable to reveal. But more important, and indeed crucial to a full understanding of the man and his work, was that he prevented me from writing about his extra-marital affairs – which served as an ersatz form of spycraft, his real operations in the field, as it were, that would last almost until his death. It introduced recurrent *sturm und drang* into what was otherwise a quiet, ordered life. Now he has died, it is important to add this coda to the biography that he encouraged, semi-authorised, and then tried to undermine.

ONE

Spying is lying

'People believe what they want to believe,' wrote David to one of his lovers. 'ALWAYS.' He was referring to the 'revelation' that Graham Greene had continued working for British intelligence into his seventies. 'No good <u>me</u> telling them that GG was far too drunk to remember anything, & that his residual connections with the Brit spooks were romantic fantasy.'

When he wrote that people believed what they wanted to believe about Greene, he might just as well have been writing about himself. People were willing to believe almost anything about him, even if he denied it (especially if he denied it) – for example, that he had once been earmarked as a possible future head of the Secret Intelligence Service (SIS, more popularly known as MI6). According to David, the Chief himself, Sir Dick White, had told him in a farewell interview that he was highly thought of within the Service; and that, had he remained, he might have been a candidate for the 'top job' in due course. This is a suggestion that one former MI6 officer, with a long and distinguished career behind him, described to me as 'ridiculous'. The idea that anyone with less than four years' experience in any organisation could be considered as a candidate to run it in due course is, to say the least, unlikely. Yet this is what David wanted us to believe. Perhaps he believed it himself.

The secret history of David's career in the intelligence services is that it was uneventful. 'The trouble with David,' observed one MI6 contemporary who served with him, 'is that he was never involved in a successful operation.'

Following his induction into MI6, and after undergoing training at Fort Monckton near Portsmouth, David was posted to Bonn, capital of what was then the Federal Republic of Germany, where he would serve out his short career, until the worldwide success of *The Spy Who Came in from the Cold* enabled him to retire and write full time. (For his last few months with the Service he relocated to the consulate at Hamburg, in an attempt to avoid the limelight.) According to a colleague who worked alongside him, there was not much for him to do there. Operations against the enemy in the East were not run from Bonn. David was working under diplomatic cover, notionally as a Second Secretary: attending press conferences and receptions with other diplomats, politicians and journalists, and escorting German politicians on visits to Britain and British politicians on visits to Germany.

David's covert role had originated in British concerns about a possible neo-Nazi revival. His perfect German allowed him to pass as a native, and he was tasked with detecting and investigating potential Nazi cells or organisations, and with recruiting German sleepers who would join such groupings in order to provide information on them. This had to be kept 'ultra secret', particularly from their German hosts, because British officials could not be seen to be interfering in German politics. But in reality there was little to do, since the feared neo-Nazi revival never materialised. Parties of the far right failed to gain mass support, and at their rallies neo-Nazis were often outnumbered by the police. David attended a few gatherings of former U-boat crews in *bierkellers*, but these were more sentimental than sinister. 'I think David was absolutely bored stiff,' wrote his Bonn colleague. The most valuable outcome of his three years in Bonn was the material it provided for his novel *A Small Town in Germany* (1968), which imagined such an extreme right-wing revival occurring in the near future.

He seems to have had more fun in his earlier career with MI5. Intelligence officers in the security service were permitted to carry out acts normally regarded as criminal: breaking and entering, burgling and bugging; as well as clandestine surveillance and 'tailing'. This appealed to David's boyish instincts. 'Hell, Jack, we're licensed crooks, that's all I'm saying,' admits one of his characters, a CIA agent, in *A Perfect Spy*.

David had been an undergraduate at Oxford when he was recruited as an MI5 asset by Vivian Green, the chaplain of his college and eventually one of the models for his most celebrated character, George Smiley. David was asked to befriend left-wing students and report on what they did. This involved an uncomfortable degree of pretence, getting close to likely undergraduates in order to win their confidence. On at least one occasion he searched a friend's rooms while he was out. He also attended meetings of left-wing societies and travelled down to London to join the sparse audiences at showings of worthy films screened at the Soviet Embassy. He was trailing his coat, hoping to attract the attention of a Soviet talent-spotter; and for a while he was courted by a 'Cultural Secretary' who then suddenly dropped him, perhaps smelling a rat.

His father's bankruptcy in 1954 compelled David to leave Oxford at the end of his second year, but he was able to return twelve months later when MI5 offered to pay his costs, funding him covertly through the local authority. In his memoir *The Pigeon Tunnel* David let drop that he had been inducted into MI5 in 1956, the year that he left Oxford to become a schoolmaster at Eton, at the age of twenty-five. Assuming this date to be accurate, it indicates that he knew he was destined for MI5 throughout the two years he spent teaching. Such deferred entry was not unusual; the Service liked recruits to have some experience of the world before joining.

David claimed that I had given an incomplete account of his covert work in my biography, though he declined to elaborate. He referred to the promises he made to his old German contacts, as well as to the Official Secrets Act. 'I am bound, legally and morally, not to reveal the nature of my work in SIS,' he wrote to me at one point. His overt role required him to cultivate German politicians and journalists, and it seems possible that he gathered intelligence as a by-product, especially on left-leaning politicians who might be suspected of having contact with figures in the East. It would have been understandable if he preferred not to admit that he had been spying on close friends – for example, on a prominent West German politician who would become godfather to one of his own sons. While refusing to be drawn, he was willing to concede that his covert role was 'negligible': he did not run agents into East Germany and never ventured there undercover himself. His penetration of the Eastern bloc was limited to a few excursions into East Berlin, each lasting no longer than a few hours, of the type available to any tourist at the time. Whatever some readers might come to believe, he was no George Smiley.

*

Working in the intelligence services often involves pretending to be something other than what you really are; and pretending to be doing something other than what you are really doing. To paraphrase a line of David's, spying is lying.

'I'm a liar,' he told two private detectives whom he had hired to investigate his life, at a time when he was contemplating some form of autobiography. 'Born to lying, bred to it, trained to it by an industry that lies for a living, practised in it as a novelist.' I spent many hours interviewing David, and while he was apparently open with me on most subjects, I quickly learned not to rely on anything he said. When he complained, as he did more than once, that I didn't always trust what he told me, I quoted his own words back at him.

Often, I am convinced, he was not trying to deceive me, but was confident in the truth of the story he was telling. On one occasion, when I was able to demonstrate to him that something he had just told me was false, he seemed genuinely unnerved. I came to appreciate that these two tendencies were consistent. He was a performer, who so inhabited each role he played that he believed it to be real. This was a valuable quality in someone who lied for a living.

David was always fascinated by Kim Philby, the Soviet double agent who penetrated so deep into MI6 that (unlike David) he was for a while a serious candidate to become its Chief when the post next became vacant. David's novel *Tinker Tailor Soldier Spy* (1974) relates the hunt for a mole who has burrowed deep into the heart of British intelligence, just as Philby had done.

David claimed a personal affinity with Philby: like him, he had a monster for a father; like him, he had served his time in institutions from which he had become alienated. 'I felt I knew him too well,' he wrote, in an introduction to an edition of *Tinker Tailor Soldier Spy*. Philby was his 'secret sharer',* who had done what David himself might have done, what Magnus Pym in fact does in *A Perfect Spy*. For Kim, as for David, 'women were his secret audience.'

> He used them like he used society: he performed, danced, phantasized with them, begged their approbation, used them as a response for his histrionic talents, as a consolation for a manhood haunted by his father's ghost. When they came too close, he punished them or sent them away ...

In the mid-1980s David would tell Sue Dawson – a member of his own 'secret audience' – that Philby had 'haunted my entire career'. Over a boozy and flirtatious lunch he related the colourful story of how he had learned of Philby's defection, while still serving with MI6 himself, stationed in Bonn. One night in January 1963, as duty officer, he had decoded a message to the effect that an officer of the Service in Beirut had suddenly gone missing. To his rapt audience over lunch, he re-enacted his own astonished reaction as the identity of the defector had become apparent: 'Christ! – it's Kim!'

Towards the end of his life David would claim that he had been 'blown' by Philby: that Philby had revealed to his Soviet handlers that David was an MI6 officer. How David knew this,

---

* A favourite phrase of David's, deriving from Joseph Conrad's novella of the same name.

he did not say. Had it not been for Philby, he implied, he might have remained within MI6, maybe even risen to the top. In a television interview given to *Channel 4 News* in 2010, David stated that his 'betrayal' by Philby was one reason why he had avoided meeting him on his visit to the Soviet Union in 1987.

By this late stage of his career David was widely regarded as a sage, his pronouncements accepted without question. But there are grounds for doubt, at least on matters concerning Philby. For one thing, it seems extremely unlikely that Philby would have been aware of David's existence when he defected in January 1963. Philby had resigned from MI6 almost ten years before David joined; and though he continued to be funded by the Service as a source while working as a journalist in Beirut, he had remained under suspicion. It was therefore inconceivable that he would have access to the names of new recruits at such a time. Though it was theoretically possible that Philby could have come across David's name as a lowly informant to the Berne SIS station in the late 1940s and have thought this information worth transmitting to his Soviet handler, this is so unlikely as to stretch the bounds of credulity. The head of the Berne station at the time, Nicholas Elliott, was a close friend of Philby's; nevertheless he would not have been so unprofessional as to share the names of his informants with anyone, not even with his chum Kim. Nor was there any conceivable motive for him to have done so.

It is impossible to prove a negative; but it is difficult to credit David's claim that he was 'blown' by Philby. The likely truth is more banal: that he blew his own cover, in the early 1980s, when he finally admitted what had long been suspected, that he had been a spy. (John le Carré's cover had been blown much earlier, in January 1964, when the *Sunday Times* 'Atticus' column revealed that the name was a pseudonym for an unknown civil servant called David Cornwell.)

David's anecdote of learning about Philby's defection as a young duty officer does not ring true. In the early 1960s Englishmen of his class addressed even close colleagues by their surnames. Would he really have exclaimed 'It's Kim!' about a man whom he had never met?

*

Towards the end of his life, as part of his research for one of his last novels, *A Legacy of Spies*, David visited the Stasi Museum in Berlin, and was given a personal tour of the Stasi headquarters. 'I had time alone in those horrible little rooms,' he later told a journalist from an Australian newspaper. 'It gave me back the smells, and the fear. And also – which, as can easily go missing – the justification for what we did. Because this was a foul regime.' He found one Berlin safe house ('much tarted up'), that he remembered from the 1960s, and located others, much to his amusement, in the Stasi files.

David was able to examine his own Stasi file, which had been obtained by the BBC as background for a documentary (in which he had originally agreed to participate, but from which he subsequently withdrew). The file had been redacted, and what remained proved to be an anti-climax, not much more than a few press cuttings and some notes on his family; there was not even any record that he had served as a diplomat in Bonn, let alone as an undercover officer for MI6. But it turned out that there was a much bulkier and more revealing Stasi file on his father, Ronnie Cornwell. From its contents David deduced that Ronnie had offered himself to the East Germans as a potential intermediary (even as his son was serving in Bonn), and that they seemed to have accepted him at face value, as a rich and successful businessman. 'I think my father conned the Stasi,' David told James Naughtie on BBC's *Today* programme in 2017.

One puzzling detail was that a Stasi agent had been dispatched to London to reconnoitre Ronnie's office in Jermyn Street, and had returned with a detailed diagram, showing the position of the telex machine and safe. David could find no satisfying explanation for this expedition. 'It's a mystery. I don't know what it means,' he told one interviewer. One expert suggests that this could have been a 'technical recce', prior to bugging Ronnie's office.

*

'Those of us who have been inside the secret tent never really leave it,' David wrote in *The Pigeon Tunnel*. 'I miss the Office, always have done – both Offices* – in their way,' David wrote to Alan Judd, another former SIS man turned novelist, in 2019. 'In a sense they are the only places, apart from writing.' He was restating a view that he had often expressed over the years, that the actions of the intelligence arms of the state reflect its true nature. He saw the secret services 'as a microcosm of the British condition, of our social attitudes and our vanities'. By the same token, the officers of the intelligence services are the only ones who know what is really going on, keeping the enemies of the state at bay so that ordinary citizens can sleep soundly in their

---

* i.e. MI5 and MI6.

ignorance. To be privy to such secret knowledge could make the possessor feel superior, someone admitted to the inner sanctum.

It suited David's purpose to suggest that spy fiction depicted the reality of a society, revealing its underside. And in his hands, arguably, that was true. But it would be equally possible to argue the opposite, that the intelligence services in David's time were out of touch with what was going on in the wider world, lost in nostalgia for past glories. That was certainly how 'the Department' is portrayed in *The Looking-Glass War* (1965), David's follow-up to *The Spy Who Came in from the Cold*.

Suggestions that the British intelligence services were incompetent and unscrupulous, recurring in book after book over the decades, angered many long-serving intelligence officers. 'You utter bastard!' one of them swore at him, in a chance encounter at an embassy reception. Only a few months after David's letter to Judd expressing how he still missed 'the Office', Sir Richard Dearlove, a former 'C' (SIS Chief), accused David of giving spies a bad name. According to Dearlove, speaking in public at the Cliveden Literary Festival, the novels of John le Carré were 'a stain' on the reputation of the Secret Intelligence Service; moreover, they were unrealistic, as they were 'exclusively about betrayal'. So 'corrosive' was le Carré's view of MI6, he went on, that 'most professional SIS officers are pretty angry with him'. One such officer, perhaps, was Daphne Park, known as the 'Queen of Spies' after her long career with MI6. 'John le Carré I would gladly hang, draw and quarter,' she told a journalist shortly before she died.

David pretended to be delighted. Dearlove's attack, he wrote, provided publicity for his forthcoming novel. 'I would have paid good money,' he claimed, for Sir Richard to 'loose off a full-frontal at me and my work less than a month before my new novel hits the stands'. He suggested that the former Chief was still bitter about the criticism he had received (from David, among others) for his endorsement of faulty intelligence in the run-up to the Iraq war. 'To this day, I am told, he continues to believe that Saddam Hussein's weapons of mass destruction were the real McCoy.' David reported that he had received an email from 'a respected former senior member of the Service', disputing what Sir Richard had said. Far from being angry with him, David suggested, his correspondent and other former colleagues were more likely to be angry with Sir Richard, for 'presiding over the flow of dicey intelligence to Mr Blair's office'.

Dearlove's attitude was noticeably different from that of his predecessor, Sir David Spedding, who had invited David to lunch at MI6's new headquarters on the South Bank of the Thames, and thanked him for what he had done for the Service's image;* and from that of Spedding's predecessor, Sir Colin McColl, who told a friend that 'the Firm likes le Carré's stuff because it makes us look so *good*'. He expatiated on the subject to the BBC's security correspondent, Gordon Corera:

> There were those who were furious with John le Carré because he depicts everybody as such disagreeable characters and they are always plotting against each other. We know we weren't always as disagreeable as that and we certainly weren't plotting against each other. So people got rather cross about it. But actually I thought it was terrific because ... it carried the name

---

* In 1997 David accepted an invitation to address one of the spouses' courses at Fort Monckton, regular briefings for new spouses of MI6 officers or those about to go abroad for the first time.

that had been provided by Bond and John Buchan ... It gave us another couple of generations of being in some way special.

After David's death, Richard Moore, the current SIS Chief, tweeted that le Carré had been 'a giant of literature who left his mark on MI6 through his evocative and brilliant novels'. He offered 'Condolences from all at the River House' – a reference to the television adaptation of *The Night Manager*, in which this term for the MI6 headquarters had first been used. Dearlove, on the other hand, renewed his offensive, now that his opponent could no longer retaliate, in an article for the *Telegraph*, restating many of the criticisms he had made at Cliveden. Dearlove asserted that le Carré had enjoyed tarring the reputation of his former colleagues in the eyes of the public. 'It was clear that he disliked, perhaps even detested, the Service that was the source of his inspiration,' he wrote.

On the contrary, David's letters to Judd suggest that he hankered after some continuing involvement with 'the Office', especially when the ambassador for the Russian Federation paid a visit to Tregiffian early in 1996. There seemed nothing to indicate that this was anything more than a social call, but David wrote as if it might be a significant opportunity for intelligence gathering, or even for a diplomatic coup. Sadly this seems to have been an old spy's fantasy.

*

Compared to the life of a spy, the life of a writer, even a bestselling writer, is a dull one. After leaving the Service at an early age, David faced a lifetime of sitting alone in his study, scribbling. There would be no more clandestine assignations, encoded communications, or secrets to be kept hidden – except his own.

David's extramarital adventures were so extensive and long-lasting as to prompt the question: wasn't all this philandering a distraction from his writing? It required considerable organisation, not to say tradecraft, with codes, false names,* dead letter boxes, and safe houses – flats where he would go and supposedly write undisturbed, in reality places where he could take women without fear of discovery. Sympathetic male friends were enlisted to act as 'cut-outs', receiving post that otherwise might be intercepted by Jane. (This system broke down when one such intermediary was admitted to hospital, leaving his wife to open an incriminating letter.) He arranged assignations abroad, booked into hotels under assumed names, used a dedicated travel agent (a former intelligence colleague, or so he told one of his lovers), and listed women in his address book under code names. In a sense he was playing at being a spy. Several of the women in his life made that analogy, deciding that he was running them like agents. The reality was that he found the secrecy stimulating, introducing jeopardy and excitement into the humdrum routine of everyday existence. More than once he took a woman to the family home when Jane was away, even sharing the marital bed, though this meant risking exposure. Far from being a distraction, his clandestine affairs became important, perhaps even essential to his writing. And just as infidelity enlivened his real life, so betrayal became the underlying theme of his fiction, the one reflecting the other.

---

* He would use the name 'Cosgrove' or 'Cosgrave' when checking into a hotel with a woman not his wife.

TWO

'My great failure to find happiness'

'They fucked us up rotten,' David wrote to his brother Tony in 2007, when he was sixty-six and Tony two years older. 'They' were their parents, Ronnie and Olive, on whom he blamed all his difficulties with love. Ronnie had been 'disgusting': rapacious, unprincipled and abusive. He had made himself rich by preying on the vulnerable, swindling old people out of their life savings and other such scams. All his life he maintained a workforce of devoted women whom he regularly discarded and revived, indulging his sexual appetite whenever and wherever he could, even molesting his own children. David's autobiographical novel, *A Perfect Spy*, had been an attempt to purge the memory of his father. 'In writing about him, I tried to make him sweeter, but it didn't work,' he wrote to Tony. After Ronnie died in 1975, 'I never mourned him, never missed him, I rejoiced at his death.' David had no doubt that his father was responsible for his failings as a husband. 'When I was faithless, I blamed him, when I promised love all over town, it was his fault ...'

As for Olive, David could not forgive her for abandoning her children when she left Ronnie – without even saying goodbye. He was never quite sure exactly when she had left, but he had been about five years old; and he would not see her again throughout all the years of his boyhood. At the age of twenty-one, he had sought her out, perhaps hoping for some kind of reconciliation with the past, but in vain. He saw her three times, and then stopped. 'I have not seen her since those rather grue-some meetings; and really find her awfully hard to tolerate at all,' he wrote in 1968, more than fifteen years after his reunion with his mother: a period during which he had become a husband, a father and a bestselling novelist. 'I found her gauche, appallingly sentimental and possessive, or pathetically guilty.'

He was still angry with his mother when he wrote to Tony in 2007, though by this time she had been dead nearly twenty years. 'I was never able to understand – I still can't even begin to – how you walk out on two sons in the middle of the night, then take the high moral ground.' In *A Perfect Spy*, his alter ego Magnus Pym writes of his mother, 'she is dead for me'. Like David, the young Magnus had tracked down his mother, and been dismayed to find, when he sees her on a station platform, rather than the pale girl wearing a cloche bonnet in the sepia photograph he has cherished through all the years of his child-hood, 'a lolloping old biddy in a pantomime hat'.

In Olive's last years, when she was an old lady in a nursing home, David paid some of her costs, and wrote her sentimen-tal letters, professing filial affection, even love. But the tone didn't ring true. 'It was all fake,' reckoned her daughter Alex, David's half-sister: 'he was acting a part.' Perhaps he was trying to assume an emotion that he didn't feel, or perhaps he was putting on a show for the staff at the nursing home. The reality was that he never forgave his mother, any more than he forgave his father. But though Ronnie had been a wicked man, he had at least been present as his boys were growing up – when he wasn't serving time in prison. David's feelings for his father were more ambiguous than he would later admit. While he despised him as a man, he could not help loving him as a parent. And his use of his father's argot suggested that he was like him in other ways too: for example, talking about serving time in the 'slammer', as if a prison sentence were something to be laughed off.

His mother's desertion left David with a lifelong mistrust of women. In his secret self, women were not to be relied upon, because they would always leave you. 'To be deprived of a young mother's love is to be deprived of all love,' he remarked in an unguarded moment to one of his few confidants. With such scars, it was difficult to lower your guard; one might say 'I love you', and not mean it. 'He kept saying it,' David has a woman say of Pym in *A Perfect Spy*: 'Like a ritual he was trying to believe in. "I love you." I suppose he thought if he said it to enough people enough times, one day it might be true. It wasn't. He never loved a woman in his life. We were enemy, all of us.'

The trajectory of his affairs was always the same: he would pursue the woman urgently, and then he would lose interest.

The women in le Carré's fiction are usually seen from a distance, which may help to explain why his novels appeal less to female readers than to male. His women tend to be thin, beautiful and unobtainable: often the possessions of a dangerous enemy, like Roper's Jed in *The Night Manager* or Drake Ko's Liese in *The Honourable Schoolboy*. They are little more than objects of desire. His more developed female characters are sexless or even grotesque, like Connie Sachs, queen of research at the Circus, described when first encountered as 'a big woman', with 'a low belly like an old man's'. (Later she becomes a sad old drunk.) Then of course there is Smiley's wife, Lady Ann, whose most distinguishing characteristic is her absence. Given that David was a serial adulterer, it seems ironic that his most celebrated character should have been a cuckold. George Smiley remains devoted to his aristocratic wife, while she takes lover after lover. Through a sequence of his novels we witness his misery at her absence and his longing for her return. Indeed, Smiley's love for Lady Ann is his Achilles heel, as his arch-enemy Karla recognises, encouraging his agent Bill Haydon to seduce her. 'He reckoned that if I were known to be Ann's lover around the place you wouldn't see me very straight when it came to other things,' Haydon confesses to Smiley, once his treachery has been exposed.

David believed that his miserable childhood explained his restless search for love. 'The only poetry we remember is the stuff we learned as kids, & it's not much different with love,' he wrote to Tony. 'You chase after it, act it, imitate it, and eventually, if you're old & lucky, you believe in it, but it comes hard, it's flawed, & we fake it a lot, like religion, in the hope that one day we'll have it for real ...'

He feared that he was damaged, perhaps broken; and that when the innermost Russian doll of his personality was opened, there would be nothing inside. And in writing about writing, he often remarked that novelists have no real centre. 'I sometimes think he is entirely put together from bits of other people, poor fellow,' Pym's friend and controller Axel says of him, towards the end of *A Perfect Spy*. Pym's former lover Kate likens him to a shell. 'All you have to do is to find the hermit crab that climbed into him,' she says. 'Don't look for the truth about him. The truth is what we gave him of ourselves.'

In a letter to his second wife, Jane, written in 1987, after they had been married for fifteen years, David expressed to her his 'immense gratitude for your secret understanding of me, and for your endless forgiveness of my inconstancies of mind & behaviour as I tried to get to the centre of myself, often at some cost to us both ...'

David often quoted the saying that an unhappy childhood was part of the asset balance of a writer – a 'dictum' that he ascribed, perhaps mistakenly, to Graham Greene – usually adding that, 'by those standards, I was a millionaire.' It is only a slight exaggeration to say that his entire writing career can be seen as an attempt to come to terms with the trauma of his early years.

'People who have had very unhappy childhoods,' he once wrote, 'are pretty good at inventing themselves.' As a boy he learned to invent, making up stories to entertain, to fantasise, escaping from reality, and to dissemble, adopting one persona to conceal another. As an adult he put these skills to professional use, first as a spy, and then as a novelist. He was a self-made man – not in the usual meaning of that phrase, though he was that too, but in the sense that he put on a show to keep the unhappiness at bay. And when David Cornwell became John le Carré, that was yet another mask to hide behind.

David worried that he had no real feelings, that he was incapable of love, that he was forever pretending. His fictional equivalents – Magnus Pym in *A Perfect Spy* or Ted Mundy in *Absolute Friends*, for example – are troubled by the sense that they don't really know themselves. As I came to know him better, I came to appreciate that beneath the witty, urbane exterior lay a man surprisingly ill at ease.

The deficiencies of his parents strengthened David's resolve to be a good father himself. It was therefore ironic that he should leave his first wife Ann, the mother of his first three sons, while they were all still children. In a note to be read by them after his death, David wrote, 'I regret more than I can say the failure of my first marriage and the pain that it inflicted on you all.'

But I knew nothing of life in those days, I had no learning in parental love, no trust in women, no identity beyond a terrible need to escape my vile childhood & be acknowledged in some way. Sometimes I can forgive myself, often not.

*

David worried that he might be like his father and struggled not to be. One of the characteristics that drew him to Ann Sharp, whom he married in 1954, was her strong moral sense, contrasting so vividly with Ronnie's venality. They were a child-like couple: he called her 'mother' and they communicated with each other in baby talk. Later he would tell Susie Kennaway that MI5 had instructed him to marry Ann as a means of infiltrating the left-wing student groups of which she was a member. But this seems to have been nonsense, one of the many stories he told his lovers that wasn't true. In a letter that he wrote to me, he claimed that he had been 'dragooned into an unhappy marriage', without explaining who had done the dragooning.

Ann was the first woman he ever slept with, in a London hotel. It seemed somehow appropriate that his first experience of sex should have occurred en route to his reunion with his mother at an East Anglian railway station. In later life David fetishised his mother's departure. After her death he reclaimed the white hide suitcase with a pink silk lining that she had taken with her all those years before, on the night she had left her sleeping boys behind.

When his first marriage was in trouble David complained to a psychiatrist that Ann resented his writing, and even tried to sabotage it by interrupting him and otherwise making it difficult for him to find the necessary time. Whether this was fair or not is unknowable. Perhaps she was jealous of his talent, as she had hoped to become a writer herself. Perhaps she felt that writing took him away from her, as arguably it did. 'It was the gradual sense of hopelessness about marriage, of utter solitude, which first drove me to write,' he would claim.

For the first eight or so years of their marriage David was faithful to Ann. His fall from grace came in the early 1960s, while he was serving in Bonn. When the wife of one of his colleagues made a pass at him at a dinner party, David reciprocated. It was a tormented love affair, consummated only once, but it was the precursor of things to come. His success as a writer of spy fiction enabled him to leave the Service and to live as he pleased; in Ann's eyes it turned his head. He began one love affair, then another; then embarked on a period of hectic promiscuity that lasted several years. As he would describe it much later, 'I was a caged animal, and with the success of my writing the door was opening.'

Perhaps the most tempestuous of these affairs was with Susie Kennaway, the wife of his best friend, though arguably he was just as much emotionally involved – and possibly more so – with her husband James. 'Jim, Jim, don't come near me for a long time, please not!' he would beg when it was over.

One of his earliest conquests was Liz Tollinton, a shy young woman who became his secretary after he lured her away from the MI5 typing pool. Though engaged to someone else when she first came to work for David, she was sexually inexperienced; in retrospect, she believed that her virginity had proved irresistible to him. Many years later he would remember her as

> very tall, big-eyed, and radiant, with a considerable intellect and a scathing wit. She possessed enormous charm of a faux-naïve kind, and an over-protected sensitivity to everything … Elizabeth had great physical grace of a ballerina's kind, and extraordinarily strong facial features, which would have delighted any painter.

He inscribed a copy of *The Spy Who Came in from the Cold* for her, 'With love from John le Carré', and added cartoons of 'Rugged Leamas' (looking much like David himself) and 'Mixed-up Liz'.*

The affair lasted six months. David soon began to find her a burden. She seemed to him neurotic: she cried down the telephone when he told her that he could not meet her, drank heavily when he was not there, and took sedatives on top of stimulants, to the extent that she once almost died. She told herself that he would marry her, and when he offered to buy her a gold charm, persuaded him instead to buy her a ring, a large, uncut stone which she wore on her engagement finger. He was relieved when he managed to get rid of her, and hired a new secretary to take her place; but, to his exasperation, she remained in contact with his wife Ann.

---

* Alec Leamas is the eponymous spy in *The Spy Who Came in from the Cold*; Liz Gold is his girlfriend.

It was never going to be easy to produce a successor to *The Spy Who Came in from the Cold*. His follow-up novel, *The Looking-Glass War*, was perceived as a failure, and he struggled to write the next one, too. It did not help that his domestic arrangements were so unsettled. On the advice of his accountant he spent several peripatetic years living out of England, first on Crete, then on Spetses, then in Vienna, never staying anywhere for long. Even after his return he was still rootless. While Ann searched for a house in the country where they could settle, he bought a penthouse flat on the thirteenth floor of a tower block in Maida Vale. In 1965 he told Ann that he was leaving her, though he returned some months later; and in 1968 he left her for good. 'I am going away to write a book and come to terms with life,' he wrote to her. He referred to 'my great failure to find happiness'.

Following the collapse of his marriage, and his turbulent involvement with the Kennaways, David was left angry and humiliated, without self-respect. He felt that he knew nothing of women, and at the same time he was deeply wary of them. 'I was ready to throw myself at anyone,' he explained to me. 'My mood-swings were awful: near-suicidal, depressions ... periods of manic euphoria, and boredom in between.'

He listed the 'Reasons' for his philandering:

1. Ever since childhood, a search for elemental creature warmth & love
2. A recognition – at 30 – that I had given my youth away to a marriage that only made me sad
3. An ignorance & suspicion of all women, a never-ending search for love; carnality, self-destruction, reckless despair, hope

4. Depression
5. No self-esteem
6. Fury at the chains of convention
7. Utter loneliness
8. Fury at my own conformity with convention
9. A root fear of women, again

His relations with Ann improved after they separated. They shared a parental concern for their three sons, particularly the youngest, Tim, who would struggle with mental illness throughout his life. But it was more than just a common interest. Two decades after they divorced, David would remark that Ann was still in love with him – 'and I suppose I'm still in love with her'. He sent her the typescripts of his books, perhaps hoping for her approval. A witness who overheard him asking her what she thought of his novel *The Tailor of Panama* (1996) likened him to 'a boy begging for the leash'.

'David, you know I don't like the picaresque,' she said.

'Yes, yes, I know.'

'It's full of your old hates. I notice you haven't left the FO.'

'No.'

'Nice characters,' she said, relenting.

'You liked Louisa?'

'Oh, I loved Louisa.'

Louisa is the tailor's wife, who searches her husband's desk for evidence of his infidelity, just as Ann had done herself, and Jane may have done in turn.

*

Perhaps it was true, as David would later maintain, that Susie

Kennaway was no more than the first in a long line of lovers. His declarations of love for her would be reproduced almost word for word in letters he would write subsequently to other women. But her husband James was the man David wanted to be: adventurous, virile, uninhibited. In trying to reshape himself he took Kennaway as a model. When she read a biography of James Kennaway, his lover Sue Dawson would notice that David had adopted some of his mannerisms and even his expressions.

David's intense friendship with James Kennaway, and his portrayal of the relationship between two similar characters in his novel *The Naïve and Sentimental Lover*, led some to imagine that he was a closet homosexual. Ann certainly suspected this. After his disastrous affair with Susie Kennaway, Ann put it to him that he had consummated a homosexual love affair with the wife of his loved one.

As a very good-looking man, David attracted attention from men as well as from women. The newly arrived Professor of Poetry, W. H. Auden, had tried to pick him up while he was still an undergraduate; when David haltingly declined the pass, the ageing poet came up with a line that David so relished that he used it twice in his novels: 'it's nice to be fancied.' There was a feminine side to David's manner which could verge on camp; as a young man he addressed his friend Robin Cooke as 'sweetheart', and on one occasion they found it expedient to leave a pub abruptly after their exuberant behaviour had led them to be taken for 'a couple of queers'. Even in middle age, according to one of his lovers, he 'giggled like a girl'. When David chose to exercise his charm, the effect was beguiling; and when he withdrew his attention it was hurtful.

David's close friendship with the homosexual artist John

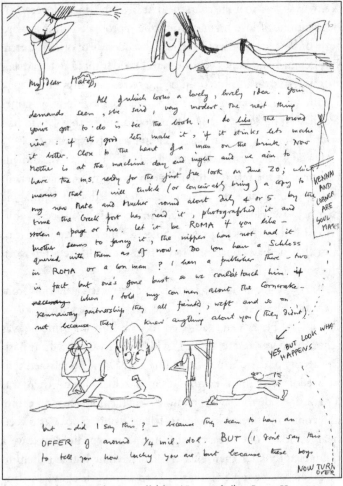

My dear Matey,

All ghoulish looks a lovely, lovely idea. Your demands seem, she said, very modest. The next thing you've got to do is see the book. I do like the broad view: if its good lets make it, if it stinks lets make it better. Close to the heart of a man on the brink. Now mother is at the machine day and night and we aim to have the ms. ready for the first free look on June 20; which means that I will trickle (or conceivably bring) a copy to my new Mate and Mucker round about July 4 or 5 by which time the Greek post has read it, photographed it and stolen a page or two. Let it be ROMA if you like — mother seems to fancy it, the nippers have not had it queried with them as of now. Do you have a Schloss in ROMA or a con man? I have a publisher there — two in fact but one's gone bust so we couldn't touch him. ~~If necessary~~ when I told my con men about the Corncrake — Kennaway partnership they all fainted, wept and so on not because they knew anything about you (they didn't).

KENNA AND CORNCRAKE ARE SOUL MATES

YES BUT LOOK WHAT HAPPENS

but — did I say this? — because they seem to have an OFFER of around ¼ mil. dol. BUT (I don't say this to tell you how lucky you are but because these boys

NOW TURN OVER

A letter from David Cornwell (alias 'Corncrake') to James Kennaway ('my new mate and mucker'), undated but written from Crete in the late spring of 1964, about the possibility of collaborating on are going to PRESSURE this boy because 10% of 250,000 is £25000 and that's something no con man in his senses is going to let slip through his fingers) SO we may have to make a deal with somebody before we go to ROMA in order to get PEACE — or do you not tolerate? This problem is not yet acute — wait till you've seen the ms.

I like REISZ. I haven't seen his films or heard of him but Sat ev Sun morn was apparently a wow so the critics said and I believe critics anyway his name ends in TWO VOWELS, like Edmonds and is therefore attractive to me.

I hope the amount of EXPOSURE in ROMA won't ruin everything. We must take care to avoid one another. Nor have I ever worked with anyone ELSE. That would be interesting. I'm not sure I've ever worked.

BUT MR ANGLESEA THIS IS A SINGE BED

'Can we have one of these scenes where they fade out a little quicker than they meant because the CENSOR is doing his NUT?

love to all your mob re made your old murderer CORNCRAKE

a film script of David's novel *The Looking-Glass War*. 'Mother' is David's first wife, Ann; the 'con men' are agents and publishers. 'Reisz' is the film director Karel Reisz, then best known for *Saturday Night and Sunday Morning*. 'Mr Anglesea' is unidentified.

David's cartoon of himself and James Kennaway.

Miller could be produced as further evidence for this belief. When David first left Ann, he sought refuge with Miller at Sancreed House, a former Georgian rectory near Penzance which in the 1960s was a sort of gay refuge. But the very fact that he felt comfortable there suggests that he had nothing to hide. And their closeness had originated in a professional relationship; Miller had been a 'mole' within the Communist Party and David his MI5 handler. It was Miller who first took David to Tregiffian, where he and his partner Michael Truscott had once lived in a derelict cottage overlooking a vast expanse of sea on the southern side of the Cornish peninsula. David was so taken with the place that he immediately began negotiations to buy it, together with the two adjoining cottages, in order to convert them into a single house. At around the same time he bought a plot of land in the Swiss Alpine resort of Wengen and built a chalet there, thus fulfilling a long-held dream.

Whether or not there was anything in Ann's theory, there was something problematic about David's relations with other men. If women were a challenge, men were rivals. Several of the women with whom he had affairs were married to friends of his; this might happen by accident once, or even twice; but with David it happened again and again. One might think that friendship with the husband would preclude a sexual interest in the wife, unless it was, perhaps, a way of seducing the friend. One such friend was James Kennaway; another was Nicholas Mosley, like James a fellow novelist, with whom David discussed his work in detail during walks on Hampstead Heath, and shared typescripts. 'He only notices women when they are married,' observed someone who knew him well.

It was a feature of David's life that he seemed isolated, with few real friends. Some of the more famous guests at his later birthday celebrations seemed barely to know him at all. He could be ruthless in his treatment of old friends, dropping them without explanation, leaving them puzzled and hurt. It was as if he did not want to let anyone get too close. His wealth became a barrier, at least to ordinary people, but it was more than that. In a letter he wrote in 1994 to Susan Anderson, another lover, David admitted to 'a terrible problem, about friendship'.

> I'm very solitary these days and hate it, mostly, but it squeezes the work out of me, even if it sometimes makes the prose too shrill, too long & too plain pompous. And I make these sudden lurches to fill the emptiness, like (in this case) asking a total

stranger* & his wife for the weekend ... for about ten minutes it looks like being the great relationship and then suddenly I'm bored stiff and get in a terrific inside rage with myself, which conversely makes me terribly polite. And then I spend the whole weekend bowing & scraping & bustling & being somebody I'm not, & when they've gone I make faces at the disappearing car, & think of all the ways I really loathe them, & for a whole day, which for me is a prison sentence, I can't write, can't look at myself in the mirror, & can't think ... my wild thoughts or my tame ones, until the big empty closes round ...

One of David's least attractive characteristics was a tendency to disparage the people around him: not just the people he worked with, like his editors, his publishers and his agents; but also other writers, friends, lovers, and even his wife and sons.

As David became older, he nurtured protégés, especially younger men with literary ambitions. In his late forties he befriended Derek Johns, a young man working in a Hampstead bookshop. Then just thirty, Johns was writing his first novel. He had seized the opportunity to mention his book to several of the well-known writers who came into the shop, but David was the only one who responded positively. 'Maybe I can help,' he said. Over supper at the Cornwells' house in Gayton Road, with Jane and their son Nick (then aged eight), they discussed the novel and the practicalities of getting it published. Over the next few months Johns became a regular guest at Gayton Road. David introduced him to a couple of agents, and to the publisher who eventually took on the book. He spoke openly

---

* The historian John Keegan.

about his own career as a writer, and in particular about the hurt he had felt at the scorn poured on *The Naïve and Sentimental Lover*. He was generous, encouraging and supportive, while Johns was pleased and flattered to be his protégé. It did occur to Johns that there might be a homoerotic element to the older man's interest in him; but if this existed, it did not manifest itself in any way.

One spring day in 1979 the two men happened to meet in the street. David told Johns that he was holding a party at his house to celebrate election night on 3 May. 'You must come,' he insisted, 'everyone will be there.' Among those expected he mentioned Melvyn Bragg, the undisputed king of British arts broadcasting. Johns expressed his gratitude but explained that he would be visiting a girlfriend in Italy; he had already booked his flight. David seemed displeased by his reluctance. 'Postpone your trip until after the party,' he urged. 'It will be good for you.' In those days, before the modern era of cheap flights, plane travel in Europe was expensive; and though Johns had bought what was known in those days as a 'bucket shop' ticket, it had still cost him the equivalent of several weeks' salary at the bookshop. In vain he tried to explain that he could not afford to change it: as they talked, David's manner became noticeably chilly. Johns did not see him again before he left for Italy. After his return, when the two men encountered one another while walking on the Heath, the conversation was brief and David's manner was cool. He never mentioned Johns' novel, which the publisher had sent him in proof. There would be no more invitations; and it was obvious that the friendship had ended.

*

In the early 1990s David met Nicholas Shakespeare, son of one of his Oxford contemporaries. The two formed an immediate rapport, despite the difference in their ages.* 'In his company, I felt exhilarated and engaged,' Shakespeare recalled. 'I found him courageous, generous, complicated, competitive, touchy, watchful, suspicious, and incineratingly honest, although perhaps not in every single instance about himself, but then who is?'

At the time Shakespeare was struggling with a dilemma: whether to give up his safe job in literary journalism for the hazardous existence of a full-time writer. He found David 'hugely supportive' at this pivotal moment. As well as writing to Shakespeare to say that he had read his first novel and believed in his talent, he offered practical help, in the form of a 'safe house' at Tregiffian, to borrow when he was not there, and to share occasionally when he was.

Shakespeare arrived in Cornwall for his first visit a few months later. The two men sat up talking until two in the morning, over tumblers of malt whisky. David had proposed that they should write separately during the day and meet in the evenings, but on the very next day Shakespeare found himself invited to join David's regular post-lunch walk along the coastal path, after which Jane collected them in the car.

For Shakespeare, this was the first of at least a dozen stays over the next twelve years, as he wrote his next two novels, *The High Flyer* and *The Dancer Upstairs*,† and a highly praised biography of Bruce Chatwin. He would usually stay for about a fortnight,

---

* Shakespeare was the same age as David's eldest son, Simon.
† Both titles suggested by David.

working hard, invariably joining David on his daily afternoon walk when he was there, and often having dinner with him and Jane, or whoever might be staying. They played pool together, or, in fine weather, croquet, with David always winning both. They would walk along the cliffs to see his neighbour, the writer Derek Tangye, or drive over to see John Miller, or another artist friend, Karl Weschke. 'I was always utterly candid with him about almost every aspect of my life,' Shakespeare later recalled, 'and he reciprocated.'

He was an exhibitionist and charmer who moulded himself according to his audience in a way that reminded me of Bruce Chatwin, of whom one friend memorably said: 'Think of the word seduction, it doesn't matter if you are male, female, an ocelot or a tea cosy.'

Shakespeare sensed that this was not a friendship that could be taken for granted. Though the two men became very close, and remained friendly until the end, David was not someone whom he felt able to ring up and have a chat with. While very open with him when they were together, David was at the same time immensely private, and guarded his privacy to a ruthless degree, frequently changing his telephone numbers to exclude unwanted callers. Shakespeare understood this ruthlessness to derive from David's commitment to writing, a quality that would become even more apparent as he came to know the older man better. 'For me, he was a model to follow, in terms of his discipline, his respect for plot, and his narrative technique.'

*

In the early 1990s David's godson Tim Geary decided to write a novel. David and Ann had become friendly with his parents around the time he was born, more than twenty-five years earlier, during a period when they were staying in Suffolk while searching for a permanent home. David had become close to Tim's father, and it was said that they 'got up to no good together' in London; though as time passed David saw less of him, as he did many of his friends, especially those who had known him when he was married to Ann. Latterly, when David telephoned the house, it was to speak to his godson rather than his old friend.

But David had proved to be a good godfather. Once Tim was old enough to travel independently he was often invited to stay with the Cornwells in London, or to accompany David to the theatre. From time to time David would present his godson with a signed first edition of his latest work, a solemn moment. As an undergraduate studying at Cambridge, Tim remembered staying with the Cornwells in Hampstead on the day that *A Perfect Spy* was published, and observing David's pleasure at reading the favourable reviews (though in public he always denied reading reviews, whether favourable or not).

A strikingly good-looking young man, Tim had begun modelling while still a student at Cambridge and had afterwards followed his luck to Tokyo, Milan and New York. By the time he had reached his mid-twenties he was wondering what to do next. 'It was because of David's presence that I had the audacity to become a writer,' Tim would write, on hearing of David's death in 2020. David was initially very encouraging and offered him the use of the Long Barn at Tregiffian to work. They agreed that David would not read what Tim wrote, but that they would meet in the afternoon for walks along the coastal path, and often for meals, just as he did with Nicholas Shakespeare. Tim adopted David's habits of rising early, always carrying a notebook, and editing what he had written earlier that day in the afternoon, often with a whisky at hand. One evening David took Tim for dinner with John Miller and Michael Truscott. While driving home afterwards, David remarked that 'if you're going to become a novelist, you're going to have to carry an enormous number of secrets'. Tim was impressed, though not certain what he meant by this. After a month or so in Cornwall, David told him that it was time to leave. Tim did not resent being asked to move on; on the contrary, he was grateful for the help in getting started, and for the glimpse of the daily life of the writer.

At first Tim had thought about writing something 'more literary', but he changed tack when a friend suggested that he should write about what he knew, in this case the glamorous world of modelling. He soon had a lucrative book deal, and in seemingly no time his book *Ego* was being hawked around Hollywood. David offered his help ('call me anytime') in shepherding him through this minefield, but rapidly cooled when he felt that Tim was going his own way. Another reason for David's lack of enthusiasm was that his friend, the film studio executive John Calley, did not think much of the book. He stopped communicating directly with Tim and allowed Jane to continue the correspondence.

When David learned that *Ego* had been taken on by Hodder & Stoughton, his own publisher, he assumed, wrongly, that his godson had used his name to gain an entrée there. (In fact Tim had obtained an introduction to the publishing house through a contact of his sister's.) David was not as encouraging as he might have been about his godson's success, particularly when he learned that it was not the kind of book he had expected. He accused Tim of 'squandering his talent'.

'I just don't know you, & that, dear Godson, is the awkward truth,' he wrote. He said that he had been unable to read his novel. This was a crushing remark to make to a young man trying to find his voice as a writer. 'He berated me for leaning into my publicity, for [succumbing to] the thrill of selling my rights to Hollywood, for not focussing on the purity of writing itself,' Tim would write more than twenty years later, in an Instagram post mourning his godfather's death. 'Our relationship was never as close again.'

After publishing a follow-up novel to *Ego*, Tim tried to write something more ambitious which failed to attract the interest of publishers. David wrote him a kind letter, which went some way to compensating for his rather brutal treatment earlier. He advised his godson not to become downhearted:

> I fear it may have been the case that your previous work acted against you & people were trained to expect one type of book & got another & didn't want it, or like it, or like being stretched, or asked to reinvent you ... I have <u>never</u> been forgiven for publishing The Naïve and Sentimental Lover ... the reviews ring in my head to this day, & my publishers were scarcely more comforting than the reviewers! So please don't regard the book as a failure or the years as wasted – nothing that has cost you so much blood & tears will have been wasted – the internal journey alone, the fights & challenges & small victories & the characters will all belong to your private armoury in the future.

DAVID CORNWELL

As from

14 June 95

Dear Tim,

Thank you for your letter. To be honest, I don't know how to answer it; if there are things you want answered. When you speak of yourself, you have such a way of advancing behind self-disparagement, as if you actually needed sympathy for being successful in a world where success is so easily for you to obtain. I'm not surprised you always love the person who isn't with you!

It's true you have it made: in the sense that, unless you go mad, you can always count on being published,

The opening page of a letter from David Cornwell to his godson Tim Geary, who had written a novel which David thought unworthy of him.

Tim abandoned fiction and made a career elsewhere. He moved to America and never saw his godfather again, though they occasionally spoke on the telephone.

*

In the late 1960s, at a publishing event in Birmingham, David met Jane Eustace, who would become his lifelong partner. 'Her first job was to help me disengage from a galaxy of inappropriate affairs that individually had no meaning for me whatever,' David wrote to me while I was working on his biography. They began living together, in her flat in Primrose Hill and at Tregiffian; and in 1972, when she became pregnant, they married.

Jane made herself central to David's life by recognising his need for stability. She became his gatekeeper, shielding him from interruptions, keeping the world outside while he wrote inside. She deflected callers as a matter of course; even his family were kept at bay. 'Put my fucking brother on the line!' Charlotte shouted down the phone on one occasion, exasperated at Jane's attempts to prevent her from speaking to him. David, and David's writing, took precedence over everything and everybody else – including Jane. She subsumed her identity in his. But the importance of his work gave her a role, even if it was only a secondary one. If not his muse, she was his helpmeet. More than that: she was high priestess in the cult of David. Her status derived from his. It worked both ways: the necessary sacrifices made his work more important, because it had become her *raison d'être*. Often she would use the first person plural, as if speaking for a corporate entity of some kind. She was his mouthpiece when there were things that he preferred not to say, or could not be bothered with. If 'John le Carré' was a business, she was its spokesperson.

Jane's worship made him an idol, and the effect on David of such adulation was not necessarily beneficial. All writers are egotists, but some are more egotistical than others. He became demanding, self-important, and unwilling to accept criticism. He told Nicholas Shakespeare that he could not write in London because of the denigration in the air. Isolated from his peers, he lacked the capacity to see himself as others did. He declined to allow his novels to be submitted for the Booker Prize, as if it was beneath him; and fantasised about winning the Nobel Prize for Literature.

According to David, Jane had been aware from the start that she would have to share him with other women. 'From early on in our marriage she determined not to interfere with that side of my life, rather to protect me from the worst, & sustain me in my writing,' he told me. Whether it was quite as he described is hard to judge. He told some of the other women in his life that he had come to an agreement with Jane; but then some of what he told these other women was demonstrably untrue. Most of the time Jane chose to say nothing. 'She didn't ask, and I didn't tell, unless it became necessary.'

Jane was in her mid-thirties when they met. Two previous affairs with married men had ended unhappily for her. She very much wanted a child; and when Nick was born he became a source of great happiness and comfort to her. In marrying David, did she accept that something was better than nothing? Was she resigned to her lot? In material terms, of course, it was a very comfortable existence. But as long as he kept writing, she could never retire; she felt obliged to continue working until almost the end of her life.

In tolerating her husband's repeated infidelities, Jane was fulfilling the cliché that when a man marries his mistress, he creates a vacancy. She had become David's mistress after she had been discarded by her former boss, George Greenfield. In an act of barely believable selflessness – or masochism – she introduced him to David, and arranged matters so that her ex-lover would become David's literary agent. She also orchestrated David's move to new publishers, her former employers Hodder & Stoughton in Britain, and Knopf in the United States.

In later years Jane allowed herself to be described as a former editor, though in fact she had worked in the rights department at Hodder and before that had been Greenfield's secretary. Since they discussed his work together privately, it is difficult to assess how much input she had into David's books. The manuscript evidence of her contributions is minimal, and anecdotal evidence suggests that she was more of a fact-checker than a collaborator or critic. She does not seem to have helped him shape the books, nor to have offered qualitative opinions on them – on the contrary, her absolute belief in the importance of his work was one of the characteristics that made her indispensable to him. Even into her eighties she remained his faithful transcriber, typing and retyping successive drafts of his manuscripts. He never learned to type himself, and before he met Jane he had employed a succession of secretaries, but she supplanted them. 'So many men fantasize about marrying their secretaries,' he remarked in a letter to his mother, 'and I, in the very best sense, did.'

THREE

Acting like a git

David's marriage to Jane in May 1972 did not bring an end to his pursuit of other women: far from it. He was forty, handsome, wealthy and vigorous, and perhaps keen to make up for lost time, after a slow start. His friend and neighbour in Cornwall, Derek Tangye (himself a frantic fornicator), would jokingly keep a tally of women that David had taken to bed: '51, 52, 53 ...' Tangye was a foil to David, reflecting back at him his fraudulent self, or the self that he feared he would one day become. Libidinous, sometimes drunken and not always clean, Tangye lived in a small and rather squalid cottage only a short walk from Tregiffian. He was the author of 'The Minack Chronicles', a series of books celebrating the pleasures of rural Cornish life, often featuring animals as characters; his books were all bestsellers, and it became a long-running joke between the two authors that his were more popular than David's. The two writers enjoyed what David would call 'an adversarial friendship', lubricated by often-refilled glasses of whisky. Unsurprisingly Jane did not care for him, but David described him as 'a wicked, adorable man'. He would deliver the eulogy at Tangye's funeral in 1996, surveying a friendship that had lasted more than a quarter of a century: he ended by saying of Tangye that he had 'loved him greatly', despite the fact that Tangye's final words to him had been 'bugger off'.

It seems that David was having an affair with another woman even while Jane was pregnant with Nick – as I discovered quite by accident at a party late one night. I found myself chatting to someone I had never met before, who immediately impressed me with his erudition, expatiating on the merits of different translations of Proust (we were both rather drunk). When I mentioned that I had written a biography of John le Carré, he told me that he knew someone whose mother had been involved with my subject. A little while later he introduced me to his friend, Natascha, who invited me to view her collection of le Carré memorabilia. Her mother, who had died some years earlier, had been a model who used the name Liese Deniz, though she had been born Norma Dennis in Sheffield, the daughter of a long-distance lorry driver. As well as being beautiful she had an ebullient personality which shaded into bipolar disorder. She had once been married to the expatriate German artist Karl Weschke, who lived in a small house overlooking the sea near Cape Cornwall, on the other side of the peninsula from Tregiffian. By the early 1970s Liese had long been separated from Weschke, and from another partner, Natascha's father, the innovative art director Tom Wolsey. She was living in a small house in Kentish Town, north London, when she began the affair with David. He gave her a pearl necklace, and on one occasion presented her with a new car, a Saab. She read manuscripts and proofs for him, and carried out basic research for *Tinker Tailor Soldier Spy*; she suggested Alec Guinness might be a good choice to play George Smiley. David called her 'lovely,

lovely Liese', or 'schoolmistress', perhaps because she tried to restrict his drinking, evident in an inscription he wrote for her in a copy of Graham Greene's *The Honorary Consul* (1973):

> I haven't read this but I guess it's the work of another of those spoilt-brat writers who get their priorities wrong, and [carve?] themselves dull lives which they can then match against their fictional selves. I seem to remember you wanted to live with him. You should. He's another ... what was I saying? He romances. And dreams. And makes a fool of himself. To prove that he's still alive. Drinks. Ages. Lies. Is alcoholic, syphilitic, pederastic, poetic.* And of course moves from one eternal relationship to another without a pause for breath. In short, he is the perfect candidate for selection as prime mate, stable/stabil companion, and total catastrophe. I'm drunk. Goodnight. Pining also. So Lys -ysistra (?)† works wonders, sometimes. I hope you had a lousy failure tonight, and I hope he read my label, and re-reads it when he's sober, cold ... 'Life is passed in the sterile and lethargic pursuit of machismo' my <u>arse</u>. And don't tell me, I <u>know</u> this is a hack book.

Love, Hack

At first David and Liese used the Primrose Hill flat for their assignations, while Jane remained at Tregiffian; but after the Cornwells bought a house in Islington, Jane found out somehow

---

* Rimbaud is said to have introduced himself as 'alcoholic, syphilitic, pederast and poet'.

† Aristophanes' *Lysistrata* is a comic account of a scheme to end the Peloponnesian War by persuading the women of the warring cities to deny their men sex.

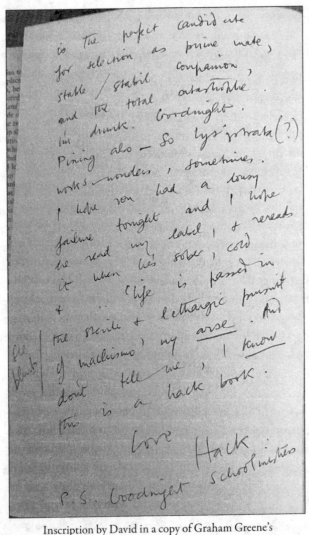

Inscription by David in a copy of Graham Greene's
The Honorary Consul, for his lover Liese Deniz.

that he was sleeping with Liese. In the ensuing confrontation, David refused to back down. He had always made it clear to her that there would be other women. 'Everybody knows that she has no money,' Jane scoffed, making the odd proposal that Liese might occupy the vacant basement flat of their new house. When David suggested this to Liese, she slammed the door in his face, 'which I rather felt I deserved!' he laughed, when telling this story some five years later.

Liese's childhood had been extraordinarily difficult; as a little girl there were signs of sexual abuse; suspicion pointed towards her violent, abusive father, though in fact a neighbour had been responsible. Her mother had stood trial for attempted murder, after she had attempted to cut her husband's throat while he was drunk; and had been acquitted only after her GP had given evidence in her favour; if he had known what she intended, he told the court, he would have directed her towards the jugular. In the mid-1950s, at the age of sixteen, Liese had left home and gone to London, changing her name and dropping her Northern accent. She had begun a successful modelling career, working for all the major fashion houses including Yves Saint Laurent, and often appearing in *Vogue*. Her story very much epitomised the social mobility of what was then known as 'Swinging London'; she mixed in both bohemia and high society, and had been publicly linked with Earl Mountbatten's son David, the Marquess of Milford Haven, before marrying Weschke in 1963. After their divorce in 1977 she would marry Lord Valentine Thynne, youngest son of the Marquess of Bath. David would use her as a model for his character Lizzie Worthington, alias Liese Worth, mistress of the Hong Kong tycoon and Soviet agent Drake Ko, in his novel *The Honourable Schoolboy* (1977).

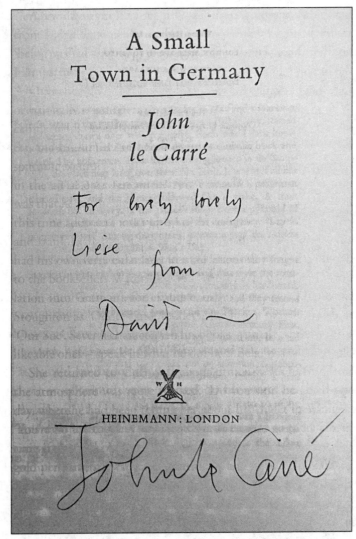

A Small
Town in Germany

*John
le Carré*

For lovely lovely
Liese
from
David ~

HEINEMANN: LONDON

John le Carré

Title page of *A Small Town in Germany*, inscribed for Liese Deniz.

*

David's relationship with Yvette Pierpaoli was unusual, in that it began as an affair and became a loving friendship, which lasted until her death in a car crash in 1999. It was also unusual in being acknowledged within the family as the latter, though not the former. They had first met in the mid-1970s, during the Cambodian civil war, at the house of a German diplomat in the besieged city of Phnom Penh, over a stylish dinner served to the clatter of outgoing gunfire from the presidential palace a hundred yards down the road. David was there investigating the background to an as-yet-unnamed novel. Yvette was accompanied by her Swiss partner, Kurt; together they ran a trading company called Suisindo, which operated from an old stucco house in the centre of town. It has been alleged that the couple were working for the CIA, which in the circumstances might have been true. Whether this could have had any bearing on what happened subsequently between David and Yvette is likewise impossible to tell.

David was fascinated by this 'small, sparky, tough, brown-eyed provincial Frenchwoman in her late thirties, by turns vulnerable and raucous, and enormously empathetic'. She would do almost anything, he wrote, 'to get food and money to the starving, medicines to the sick, shelter for the homeless, paper for the stateless, and, just generally, in the most secular, muscular, businesslike, down-to-earth way you could imagine, perform miracles'. He admired her irrepressible energy and her huge heart, which seemed big enough to embrace all the world's children. Not least of her qualities that he enjoyed was her appetite for danger. It seems too that she was attracted to him from the start, as she recalled in this draft for a memoir, which she sent to him and which I found in his correspondence.

> I see him at the house of his friend Baron von Marschall: tall, suave, charming. The open generous expression, a slight otherworldliness, his salt and pepper hair was immensely appealing. But there was also something else, which lay in the play of his mouth, the crease in his brow, or his unruly eyebrows, which said so far and no further. Seeing this, I asked myself – should I approach him, or keep my distance? I normally feel comfortable and confident around people, but when his gaze turned on me, I felt completely naked, utterly powerless. At the same time vulnerable but safe, because of his total honesty. It came over me like an attack of vertigo. I knew there could be no dissembling with this man. With him truth was everything.*

Almost twenty years after this first encounter she recalled 'this new *tendresse*', and 'the intensity of the days that followed'. The available evidence does not show whether their affair began then or later, simply that it took place in this period. Yvette never spoke publicly about her affair with David. Her daughter burned his letters after her death, in the kitchen sink, while he also destroyed most of hers; much of the story has to be reconstructed from second-hand accounts. Nevertheless it seems clear that he was in love with her, at least for a while. Much later he would tell another lover that he had been ready to leave Jane for Yvette, who had persuaded him not to. Over the next few years,

---

* This remark is perhaps only explicable in terms of relations between the two of them.

they would meet whenever David returned to Southeast Asia while continuing to research the book that would be published as *The Honourable Schoolboy* in 1977. After the fall of Phnom Penh to the Khmer Rouge in 1975, Kurt and Yvette had moved to Bangkok and tried to start up Suisindo again, but then Kurt died, and the business ran into problems; and eventually Yvette had consigned it to a manager and headed for Europe: 'determined' (as David would later write) 'to give the rest of her life to the deprived peoples of the world'.

It seems that the sexual aspect of their relationship was never very important to her and did not last long. Her feelings for him remained strong, however. She addressed him as 'Dearest David' or 'Dear exceptional and wonderful David' in her letters, which contained frequent endearments. '*Tu es un type FOR-MIDABLE*,' she wrote to him in 1984. Almost a decade later she would try to articulate how she felt about him:

> I've known him now for nearly twenty years and, during that time, he has become part of me. 'What would David say in this situation? What would David do if he were me?' These are the kind of questions I would ask myself all the time. I wanted to be like him, in the way that he seemed to understand everything, the way he loved without becoming too involved, knowing how to give without bankrupting himself.

David introduced Yvette to Jane as a friend, with no suggestion that she had ever been anything more. Jane seems to have been aware of what had happened between them, and to have accepted it as something that was past and no longer any threat to their marriage, if it ever had been. (There would be a photograph of Yvette hanging on the wall in Jane's study when she died.) Yvette often went to see them when she was in England, and particularly enjoyed visits to Tregiffian. But in 1999, while on a mission to provide aid to Kosovan refugees, Yvette died when the car she was travelling in plunged down a precipice, falling several hundred feet. Jane accompanied David to the funeral service, held at the farmhouse near Uzès in southern France where Yvette had lived, in the sense that she lived anywhere. He wept throughout the ceremony, and afterwards Yvette's close friends and even her own daughter took him aside to tell him privately that he had been the love of her life.

Before she died, David had teasingly informed Yvette that the heroine of his next book would be somebody as impossible as her. Though Tessa Quayle, the heroine of *The Constant Gardener*, would differ from Yvette in age, nationality and occupation, she would be imbued with Yvette's commitment to helping the poor and friendless, and with her dogged determination in doing so. The novel would be dedicated 'For Yvette Pierpaoli, who lived and died giving a damn.' A piece he wrote about her for the *New Yorker* was headed 'The Constant Muse'.

*

Early in 1977 a young American woman started working for the Cornwells, soon after they moved from Islington to Hampstead. Sarah (not her real name) began as a cleaner, having answered an advertisement in *The Times* from an agency offering temporary work. She came from a troubled family in the American Midwest. She knew almost no one else in England, where she had come to audition for a scholarship at RADA. Only twenty-two, and fresh out of college, she was eager for experience, and aspired to write screenplays and a novel. I came across letters from her in David's correspondence files at Tregiffian while I was working on the biography. Much later, David's friend William Shawcross put us in contact, and we spoke several times on Zoom. She sent me an account of her relations with David, on which the following passage is founded. I have no reason to doubt her testimony, but here and elsewhere, readers should bear in mind that memory is fallible, and that verbatim recall may not always be accurate.

Within hours of beginning work for the Cornwells Sarah had established a rapport with their son Nick, then just four years old and attending a local Montessori school. Jane asked Sarah to look after him as an au pair, and persuaded her to move in with them to save money. 'We always said that we'd never have another au pair, but you might just work,' she added. The meaning of this remark became obvious when Jane found a photograph of the previous au pair and tore it up. David would later tell Sarah that her predecessor had flirted with him.

At first Sarah found David (then preoccupied with revising *The Honourable Schoolboy*) remote. On only her second or third day she was mocked for not knowing that his character of 'Karla', the Soviet spymaster, was a man, not a woman. She was therefore surprised to hear from Jane that David liked her; 'he doesn't like many people.' Sarah's literary ambitions soon became conversational fodder at the Cornwells' dinner table. 'Write about me,' David urged her, in a mocking tone, with a grand wave. 'Libel me to the limit. I don't care.' Tim, David's youngest son by his first marriage, who was eating with them, rolled his eyes at her. Both knew that this was the last thing that David wanted.

Living in the house, Sarah became aware of tensions between her employers. Jane resisted David's attempts to persuade her to take a part-time job in publishing, and she often complained to Sarah about David's research abroad. So far as Jane was concerned, David could just stay at home and 'make it up!' Even Sarah, green as she was, doubted this. When Jane protested to David about one of his upcoming trips, he growled, 'It comes with the territory,' with a stern stare that indicated that he did not want to discuss the subject further. While he was abroad, and Jane again grumbled to Sarah that he did not need to go away to gather material for his books, Sarah asked if all David's travel was hard on the marriage. 'Oh, no, no, that was all with Ann! He's learned his lesson!' Jane replied brightly.

Sarah had been with the Cornwells only a few weeks when the whole family decamped to Tregiffian. It was agreed that David would drive down with Sarah and their sheepdog Smith as passengers, while Jane would follow with Nick by train the next morning. They chatted freely during the long drive down. David's mood was playful, even subversive. By the time they arrived at Tregiffian they had already achieved a degree of intimacy. 'Wouldn't it be wonderful if they never came?' he said, referring to his wife and son. Sarah ignored the remark, though she felt the same. Over lunch *à deux* on that first day, David put down his knife and fork deliberately and began to speak. 'Nothing can happen now, because there would be too many victims,' he declared, 'but someday I intend to have a long affair with you.' After Jane arrived and Nick had gone to bed, the three of them sat down to dinner, and David tried to play footsie with Sarah under the table, which sent her into a panic. As she often did, Jane retired to bed early, leaving the two of them alone. Sarah pushed away an advance from David and went to bed in the annexe leading from the kitchen, locking the door behind her; later she heard the handle being tried. When they were alone together the next morning, David told her that she had been right to resist his advances. To have an affair now would be 'nuts'.

In the days that followed they seized opportunities to be alone together, setting out on walks separately and then meeting when out of sight of the house. By the time they returned to London they were desperate for some time to themselves. They established a dead letter box for correspondence at the address of his friend John Miller, and a 'fallback meeting place', a bench on Hampstead Heath overlooking one of the duck ponds.

David was due to travel in Europe for work, which offered an opportunity for them to be alone together. Sarah told Jane that she wanted to visit friends of friends in Glasgow. She and David arranged to meet in Bruges, arriving early one afternoon. Unfortunately the bedrooms in the fifteenth-century canal-side hotel that David had chosen were small, with low ceilings; the bed took up almost all the available space. David grabbed her hand. 'We are not animals,' he breathed. Then he flicked up the index finger of his other hand into the air and announced, 'We will have lunch!'

David had reserved a table at a smart fish restaurant nearby, which embarrassed Sarah, who felt underdressed. But David was too busy to notice, ordering a seafood tower and insisting on a magnum of champagne.

While they were in Bruges David tried to persuade Sarah that she should give up acting school to concentrate on becoming a writer, discussions that continued back in London. He offered to fund her to work on a novel that she had been planning.

Meanwhile David became increasingly concerned about Tim, who was a boarder at Westminster School. The headmaster came to dinner to discuss with the Cornwells whether Tim might be happier as a day boy. The problem was that Ann was then living abroad, so the only practical alternative was for him to move in with David and Jane. One day, when David and Sarah were romping happily on Hampstead Heath together with Nick and the dogs, David took her hand and blurted out that she would make a wonderful mother. Later Sarah would interpret it differently, but at the time, she took him to mean that he wanted to set her up in a flat and start a second family with her. This was not what she wanted.

The Cornwells returned to Tregiffian for the spring holidays, taking Sarah with them. David seemed stressed and in a foul mood much of the time. On a walk they took together David told Sarah that he didn't believe anything she'd told him about her past. Shocked and upset, she suffered a miscarriage a few days later. She hadn't told him that she was pregnant, fearing he would think that she had become so deliberately. By this time she was sinking into a deep depression, and insisted on leaving to go back to America. They agreed that he would join her there soon for a month or more, 'to see your world'; but in the event they would spend only a few days together, in a New York hotel where David had reserved two separate rooms, in case Jane telephoned. Sarah spent much of the time alone, while David was out with his American editor* or attending publishing parties.

The end of the affair was messy. David returned to England

---

* Bob Gottlieb, le Carré's editor from 1970 until 1987, when he left Knopf to become editor of the *New Yorker*.

and then left on a family holiday to Greece. It seems that he misunderstood a letter Sarah had written to him; by the time he returned from holiday, there had been no contact between them for weeks. In September *The Honourable Schoolboy* was published, and David's face was on every news stand in America. Depressed, Sarah flew back to London and called him from the airport. They drove down to Tregiffian together, but it was not a happy stay. On the drive back, David accused her of wanting to sell his secrets to the newspapers; though he immediately retracted the allegation, it left a bitter taste. She left London again for the West Country, moving to St Ives to work on her novel, but by now she was in an emotionally fragile state. She found it difficult to reach David on the telephone, and when she did succeed, he 'acted like a git'. After a few weeks she decided to return to America. There she received a 'with the best will in the world' letter from David. She sent him a notebook, in which she suggested that he had been running her like 'a little girl spy'.

Sarah returned to London the following spring. She continued to walk on the Heath, where she occasionally glimpsed David. On one occasion she tried to talk to him, wanting to clarify things between them, but it all came out wrong. Eventually he lent her the money to return to America. Over the next few years there would be further letters and phone calls, which dwindled and eventually stopped.

*

After the Cornwells moved to Hampstead in 1977 they became friendly with the novelist Nicholas Mosley and his wife Verity, who lived nearby in a large double-fronted house in Church

Row. Some of Mosley's books had been published by Hodder & Stoughton, which was how he had come to know Jane. Nicholas, a hereditary peer who had inherited the title Baron Ravensdale through his mother's side of the family, was the eldest son of Sir Oswald Mosley, the notorious leader of the British Union of Fascists. In 1982 he would publish the first of a critical two-volume biography of his father, who had died two years earlier.

The two novelists formed the habit of exchanging manuscripts and discussing their work together during walks on the Heath and elsewhere. Nicholas was eight years older than David. He had fought in the Rifle Brigade in the Second World War and had been awarded the Military Cross. Like David, he had been married before, and had several children by his first wife, whom he had divorced in 1974. In that same year he had married Verity, a woman eighteen years his junior, who had worked as a fashion buyer and would later train to be a psychotherapist. Like the Cornwells, they had a young son. Both Nicholas and Verity had undergone psychoanalysis. Verity complained that he was too absorbed in his writing, 'the mistresses in his head'. In the early 1980s their marriage was going through a difficult period, with the result that for a while Mosley had moved out of the main house into a cottage in the garden. Verity had begun divorce proceedings, though Mosley had resisted these.

Mosley's early success as a novelist had stalled. His novel *Natalie Natalia* was in some ways comparable with David's *The Naïve and Sentimental Lover*, both in its themes of adulterous love and the trials of early middle age, and in its confusing narrative. Both novels were published in 1971, and both were chastised by the critics; but whereas David's career had since taken off, Mosley's had not. Like James Kennaway, he had turned to writing film scripts, but the films had not been a success. His 1971 novel was followed by what the author himself called 'an almost unpublishable book'. Not surprisingly Hodder turned it down. In 1979 it was published by Secker & Warburg. Secker's managing director, Tom Rosenthal, commented later that 'Mosley's fiction was never an easy sell'. (Notwithstanding this, Mosley remained committed to his work, and would reap his reward in 1990 when his novel *Hopeful Monsters* was awarded the Whitbread Prize.)

David, on the other hand, had become one of the most prominent authors in Britain in the decade following the relative failure of *The Naïve and Sentimental Lover*. He had returned to spy fiction with a sequence of novels featuring his most celebrated character, George Smiley, beginning with *Tinker Tailor Soldier Spy* (1974),* followed by *The Honourable Schoolboy* (1977) and *Smiley's People* (1979). The hugely successful BBC Television adaptation of *Tinker Tailor Soldier Spy* brought David's work to an even wider audience, and this would be followed in 1982 by an almost equally successful television adaptation of *Smiley's People*. His next novel, *The Little Drummer Girl* (1983), set against the background of the conflict between the Israelis and the Palestinians, promised to sell in even larger numbers, especially in America. But David was peeved when Mosley told him, on a long walk they took together, that he felt his work had taken the wrong direction. Perhaps Mosley made his low opinion of spy fiction obvious; he was committed to novels of ideas. This was a subject about which David was sensitive; and he still smarted from the critical battering he had received on

---

* David gave Mosley a copy inscribed 'For Nick, with fond wishes'.

the publication of *The Naïve and Sentimental Lover*. He never spoke to Mosley again.

Mosley later ascribed David's reaction to being unable to cope with anything other than praise from a fellow writer. He remembered only when it was too late being warned that David was in the habit of seducing the wives of his close friends. Verity was living alone, and understandably irritated with her husband for maintaining contact with a former lover. She and David began an affair. She was an attractive and intelligent woman; but on his side revenge seems to have been at least one of his motives – and Mosley himself certainly thought so. On her side it may have been no more than an understandable desire to even the score. After the affair had run its course the Mosleys' marriage would recover, and they would live together more or less equably until his death in 2017.

A few of David's love letters to Verity have survived, mostly undated so it is difficult to be sure of their sequence, but the overall pattern is clear. They met whenever they could do so discreetly. She stayed with him in Cornwall and accompanied him on trips abroad, including one to the chalet at Wengen. On at least one occasion they spent the night together in a Heathrow hotel room before he caught a flight the next morning. He gave her jewellery. His expressions of love alternated with bulletins on his progress with his new novel, *The Little Drummer Girl*. 'My love, I miss you very much, love you very much, and I write all day in a kind of driven frenzy,' he wrote in an undated letter from Tregiffian, 'and you must, must, <u>must</u> be patient of my efforts because without the bloody book there is no resolution ...'

In late May 1982 they met in Istanbul, after he had been on a research trip to Israel. 'I think my book is terribly moving,' he had written to her beforehand: 'Anyway it had <u>me</u> in tears.' They stayed at the Pera Palace, a grand hotel overlooking the Bosphorus. On an excursion into the surrounding countryside they seem to have strayed into a forbidden area and were detained and questioned by soldiers. David was very anxious, though Verity was not sure whether this was because of the potential reaction of his former employers or the possible publicity that might arise if a famous author was found to have been staying with a woman not his wife, and the consequent damage to the reception of his forthcoming novel. In his mind she and the book were entwined:

> My darling love, dearest [Verity], I have been reading Charlie's book* all day & it is so much you it is amazing – every paradox & touch & embrace, full of [Verity], every daft bit of courage, every smile. Two–three days of you, then half term, then the total solution – never mind what recent rotten things we have endured: the book is such a triumph of what you gave me, such a celebration of what you mean to me.

He gave her a copy of the typescript and seemed disgruntled when she was slow to respond. The end came in the autumn of 1982, after Jane discovered one of Verity's boots in the Cornwells' car. She had been suspicious for some months beforehand.

David tried to break it off, then relented, and Verity too seemed uncertain whether she wanted it to continue. After agonised talks on the telephone, he steeled himself to the decision a month later:

---

* The eponymous 'little drummer girl' is named Charlie.

... there is no compromise, there is only choice; and the pain of trying to pretend otherwise is terrible for both of us ... And the choice is within me; within my own nature, which is where my prison is. Who is my jailor is secondary: the prison is me, and the spells cast by my own childhood, and by so much cowering before ferocious forces; and the issue is where I can break out, whether I have the strength & the conviction ...

I have walked round it and round it, contemplated breaking all the camps, tried in my own mind again and again to fit the children into new schemes that would work ... And I have tried to persuade myself that I need nothing of Jane, nothing of the present apparatus; but the truth is, again, that I can't persuade myself ...

You gave me the heart of my book; and a great burst of hope and happiness and love ... I love you and will keep you in my heart as my best, best love ... Oh my darling love – forgive me.

*

Towards the end of 1982, when *The Little Drummer Girl* was finished but not yet published, David flew back to Lebanon. He had been there several times over the past few years to undertake research for the book; on this visit he had come to scout for possible film locations, accompanied by the director George Roy Hill and the screenwriter Loring Mandel. They were shown around by Janet Lee Stevens, a young American journalist and human-rights advocate, then working with Amnesty International, who had agreed to act as their guide and interpreter. Stevens, who had lived in Tunis and in Egypt before coming to Lebanon, was fluent in Arabic, and had become a fierce advocate of the Palestinian cause. Some suspected that she was working undercover for the CIA, but in such a febrile environment as Beirut in the early 1980s, any American was suspect. The Palestinians themselves seem to have trusted her: indeed, to have adopted her as one of their own.

Back in the summer, when Beirut was under siege from the Israeli Defence Force, Stevens had pleaded with Yasser Arafat not to withdraw his Palestinian Liberation Organization (PLO) fighters from Lebanon. She urged him not to trust American guarantees to protect Palestinian civilians in the refugee camps. 'Women and children are terrified of what might happen if their husbands and brothers leave them alone.' She had become tearful and distraught; the Palestinian leader had wrapped his arms around her, as she beat his shoulders with clenched fists. But three weeks later he had gone, taking his fighters with him. Within a month her worst fears had been realised: during a three-day massacre of civilians in the Sabra and Shatila refugee camps by militiamen from the right-wing Phalange Party, troops of the Israeli Defence Force stood idly by. She had visited the camps immediately after the massacre, and witnessed ghastly sights: decapitated bodies, women who had been raped and then butchered, castrated boys, and slaughtered infants hurled onto rubbish heaps. Afterwards, when she happened to see one of the Phalange leaders in the street, she had marched up to him and screamed, 'Butcher!'

Stevens took David and his companions to Sabra and Shatila. Though horrified by what she told him, David admired her passion and her commitment, her courage and her heart. As he put it afterwards, these 'became the window through which we perceived the landscape she knew so well'. He joked to her that when she became old she would acquire the venerability, if not piety, of a Mother Teresa. He sympathised with the Palestinians, as he did with ordinary Israelis, though not so much with their leaders. Earlier in the year he too had been taken to meet Arafat, a clandestine rendezvous to which he had been led blindfold.

I first heard about Janet Stevens from Loring Mandel, whom I interviewed over the telephone. I heard of her again from another lover of David's, Sue Dawson. Later I discussed her with the journalist and biographer Kai Bird, whose book *The Good Spy* is a biography of Robert Ames, like Janet killed in the bombing of the American Embassy in Beirut. I met Kai at the National Book Festival in Washington, where he chaired a panel about spies and spy-writing on which I was one of the speakers.

Though there is no evidence for this, it seems possible that David met Janet Stevens on one of his previous trips to Lebanon. If so, this could help to explain an apparent anomaly. According to Kai, Janet was known to the Palestinian refugees as 'The little drummer girl', the title David adopted for his novel. Some doubt has been expressed as to whether he did really take the title from her, not least because the book was finished by the time he went to Lebanon in the autumn of 1982. It has been suggested that he was contemplating such a title back in the late 1970s, before he even began work on the novel. Whatever the truth about this, it is known that he had drawn on both his sister Charlotte and his lover Verity Ravensdale for the character of the eponymous heroine. Perhaps he drew on all three.

Whether or not she was the inspiration for the book, it seems likely that at some stage Stevens and David had become intimately involved, though he was twenty-one years her senior. 'She was just a little plain bit of a thing,' David would remark later, 'but she was a wonderful lover.'

Janet was killed, together with sixty-two others, in the explosion which wrecked the American Embassy in Beirut, on 18 April 1983. Only twenty minutes before the blast, she had arrived at the embassy to press for more aid to the Palestinians in the refugee camps. She had been sitting at a table in the cafeteria when a pickup truck packed with explosives had crashed through the embassy doors, coming to rest in the central lobby. The driver had detonated his cargo, resulting in a huge explosion that ripped through the building, causing its central wing to collapse. An Iranian-backed militia claimed responsibility for the attack.*

Later that same year David would confide to Sue Dawson that he had planned a holiday with Janet, and that they had been due to meet on the day following the bombing; he had been waiting to meet her off the short flight from Lebanon at Larnaca airport in Cyprus when he learned the terrible news of her death. In his telling, he was approached by two uniformed men, who took him to a back room and told him that the person he was waiting for had been killed. This account is to some extent corroborated by a witness who says that David flew into Beirut two days after the explosion, checked into the Commodore Hotel, and visited the ruins of the embassy. Later he flew to Atlanta to attend Janet's funeral. The film of *The Little Drummer Girl*, released in 1984, was dedicated to her memory. This caused Jane to accuse David of being her lover, which he denied absolutely.

But doubts remain about what really happened. The Beirut

---

* The veteran Beirut journalist Said Aburish told Kai Bird that 'there was a strange love affair behind the bombing', referring to David and Janet Lee Stevens.

embassy bombing made headline news around the world; could David really have been unaware of it as he waited at Larnaca airport a day later? The American academic and civil-rights lawyer Franklin Lamb, who considered himself Janet's partner, has written that he was on his way to see her in Beirut when she died, and had spoken to her on the telephone the day before. It is difficult to understand how his account can be reconciled with David's. Perhaps David fabricated at least parts of his story, in order to impress Sue Dawson? Was his story about waiting to meet her another fiction, a piece of self-dramatisation? He told Dawson that Janet had gone to the embassy on that day on his behalf – in other words, that he had been unwittingly responsible for her death. Other accounts suggest that she went there for a purpose unconnected with David.

A further twist to the story is that Janet was pregnant when she died. Whether or not David was aware of this fact is not known, though it seems likely that it would have been mentioned at her funeral. If he did become aware that she was pregnant, did he imagine the child might have been his? If so, this would have been a further desperately sad secret that he was forced to keep to himself.

FOUR

The love thief

One morning in September 1982 David met a tall, blonde, bespectacled young woman, then in her mid-twenties and living in Chelsea. Sue Dawson worked as a freelance television researcher and abridged books for audio release on cassette tapes, which in the early 1980s were experiencing something of a boom. She described herself then as 'generally up for anything'. I first met her in 2013, after a tip-off from a literary agent who had been prevented from selling a memoir of her time with David by the threat of legal action. I found her intelligent and perceptive, and of course it was fascinating for me to hear about her experiences with 'Himself', as she usually referred to him. We exchanged emails and met a couple of times in London, and once near where she lived in Durham. More often we spoke on the phone. To some extent we had experiences in common, and of course we were able to discuss David in a way that I could not easily do with anyone else. In our struggles with David we were comrades-in-arms, and we became, as she put it, chums.

In 2022, two years after David's death, she would publish an account of their subsequent affair, under the pseudonym Suleika

Dawson:* a play on Max Beerbohm's *Zuleika Dobson* (1911), a novel about a young woman who was literally a *femme fatale*, so devastatingly attractive that droves of Oxford undergraduates commit suicide out of hopeless passion for her; and perhaps also a nod to Goethe's *Book of Suleika*.† Her memoir,‡ which she tells us is based on David's letters as well as her own diaries and notebooks, makes it possible to provide a detailed narrative of their affair, and an insight into his state of mind while writing what many consider his finest novel.

They met when David came into a studio in Broadwick Street in Soho to record *Smiley's People*, which had been published three years earlier. (An adaptation of *Smiley's People* starring Alec Guinness was then being screened on BBC2.) It was unusual for an author to record his own work, as most lacked the necessary skills; then, as now, most books were read by professional actors. But David's literary agent George Greenfield had assured the production team that he was an exception, as indeed he proved to be. He was not just as good as any actor; he was better. The only problem was that he read his work more slowly than expected, with the result that Sue was obliged to make further cuts as the recording progressed, and then overnight, as David agreed to return the next morning to finish off.

Once the recording was done he inscribed a presentation

---

* 'Suleika's' cover was blown by Richard Kay in an article for the *Daily Mail*, 'Spies, lies and non-stop sex', 8 October 2022.
† A sequence of poems depicting an adulterous love affair.
‡ *The Secret Heart: John le Carré: An Intimate Memoir* (2022). Some readers may be sceptical about Dawson's ability to recall conversations. Nevertheless her record of what David said usually rings true.

copy of the book for her, with the dedication 'For lovely Sue, who shortened it ...' Then they enjoyed a long and flirtatious lunch at a Soho trattoria. In the end-of-term euphoria both were exhilarated. He ordered champagne and quizzed her about her life and boyfriends. He learned that she was an Oxford graduate, as he was himself; she had read English at Somerville. On a card he scribbled a list of books that he pressed her to read: 'they're important to me.' (To suggest a reading list to a young woman he had only just met seems an oddly egocentric gesture.) He complimented her on her work on the abridgement: 'I think I shall appoint you my Recording Angel.' Before the food arrived, he reached across the table and began to stroke the back of her hand; then he lifted it to his lips and kissed the tips of her fingers. Afterwards they hesitated about whether to go to see a film together, before strolling arm-in-arm down to Piccadilly Circus. There David hailed a passing taxi. As it drew up alongside them he kissed her urgently on the mouth, climbed into the cab, and was gone. She would not hear from him again for almost a year.

Eleven months later David returned to the studio to record his novel *The Little Drummer Girl*, which had been published earlier in the year. He seemed low. 'It was a rough summer,' he answered when asked about it. 'The thing is, I don't think I'm going to write again.' But the recording was as faultless as the first, and as it progressed he opened up; on successive days he treated Sue and Graham Goodwin, her boss at the studio, to lavish lunches, dazzling them with witty anecdotes and perfect parodies of people he had known. Goodwin seemed as smitten as she was by his performance. The meals were washed down with plenty of champagne, which he referred to as 'shampoo'.

(He used such old-fashioned slang with a kind of playful irony.) When Goodwin left the table for a moment David asked her softly if she would have dinner with him the next day, and she said yes.

He was then fifty-one, almost exactly double her age; but Dawson had already shown a penchant for older men; she had dated and been briefly engaged to someone even older than David, the comedy writer Jeremy Lloyd.* She was excited by the prospect of a romance with this attractive, clever, fascinating man.

On the Friday evening they met for drinks in a cocktail bar, followed by dinner in a restaurant; afterwards they took a taxi to his house in Hampstead, where he had been staying alone. She noticed that he asked the taxi to drop them a few doors short and waited until the driver had gone, her first observation of his tradecraft. David opened the front door and led the way to his student son's bedroom, where he had changed the sheets in anticipation of her arrival. 'We're here at last,' he said to her as he turned the Anglepoise lamp to face the wall. 'I can't believe it. Oh, *my darling*!'

In the morning they set out for an early stroll on Hampstead Heath. She asked him if he was serious about not writing any more. 'I think I might be,' David replied solemnly. He explained what had happened in the summer. 'I met someone after you, out in Lebanon, when I was researching *Drummer Girl*.' This was Janet Lee Stevens; he told her the terrible story of her death. 'We should've gone to that movie, you and I,' he said grimly. 'We really should.'

---

* Dawson does not tell us whether David relished following on from the writer of *Are You Being Served?*

But the next morning he telephoned her in ebullient mood. 'You're a miracle worker, my darling,' he exclaimed: 'You've got me writing again!' Later that day he telephoned again. Over dinner the previous Friday she had mentioned that at the end of September she would be holidaying on the Greek island of Lesbos, where some friends had lent her a house. He had already imagined her walking naked out of the sea; now he asked if he might accompany her there. On Lesbos, he told her, he would write and they would make love; he began to refer to the forthcoming trip as their 'honeymoon'.

It seemed that scenes from *The Little Drummer Girl* were being filmed on location on the nearby island of Mykonos, 'so after our trip I might go and see how they're doing.' (Perhaps this was a convenient cover story to explain his absence from home.) His son Stephen was to accompany the crew as official stills photographer.

On the following Wednesday, he telephoned again, and was disconcerted to find that she had not received several letters he had sent her in the meantime. It turned out that he had encoded her address in his address book before misreading his own code. She wondered what it must be like to feel that you needed to take precautions against being spied upon, even in your own home.

Before they left for Lesbos they spent three days together at a grand hotel in Vitznau, on the shore of Lake Lucerne in Switzerland. Their room opened onto a terrace, with views across the water to the mountains beyond. While they quaffed champagne he presented her with a small red box containing an antique gold necklace set, with garnets arranged as petals.

After their return from Switzerland David sent Sue enormous

bouquets of flowers, plus another list of recommended books; as before, he seemed to want her to read them as a means of understanding him. One of the books that he had pressed on her at their first meeting was Ford Madox Ford's *The Good Soldier*, which he described as 'the book of my life'.*

He wanted her to join him on a trip to Munich, but decided at the last minute to go alone. Nevertheless she accompanied him to the airport, so that they could at least spend a night together in a Heathrow hotel. When the taxi driver taking them there had asked where he was heading, David told him 'Oslo', before whispering in her ear, 'If you're going south, tell them north'; though why he should need to mislead a taxi driver as to his destination she failed to understand.

'I've never let anyone this far in,' David told her, quite early in their affair. 'You are safe to love, aren't you, Sue?' he asked. 'I need you to be safe.' Presumably he was asking whether she was discreet, though it was also the kind of question that a protective agent-runner might ask. When she asked him what he would do if Jane ever found out about their affair, his answer was unequivocal: 'I'd deny you – I would deny you utterly.'

He had an odd way of talking to her in the third person. 'Would a girl like to go out to lunch?' he would ask. This failure to address her by name suggested that she was anonymous, one of a succession of lovers.

They arranged a rendezvous at the airport in Zurich, to fly

---

* Edward Ashburnham, 'the good soldier' of the book's title, is a passionate and sentimental man who causes his wife pain and humiliation by repeated infidelity. In *A Perfect Spy* Magnus Pym has a copy of *The Good Solder*, which he 'reads incessantly these days; it has become his Bible'.

on together to Greece. As usual he had made the bookings with a private travel agent who, so David said, had worked in intelligence. He had instructed 'my spook travel agent' that 'no one can know about us', he told Sue. It seemed that David always flew by Swissair, and he used an American Express card provided by his Swiss literary agent Rainer Heumann for all his trips and treats. Heumann seemed the sort of person who might have been some kind of spy, and David indicated that his British literary agent George Greenfield had worked in military intelligence.* David seemed surrounded by 'spooks'.

She observed that when they were out in public together he was always watchful, scanning the exits and entrances at the airport, for example. He did not relax until they reached their destination, because, as he later explained to her, 'they could still get us before we do.' Sue began to feel that he was running her like an agent in the field. How much of this was real? Was David Cornwell playing at being John le Carré?

They took a taxi from the airport at Lesbos to the port of Plomari. The little house her friends had lent her was a few hundred yards up the hill from the harbour. 'Oh my darling, *look*,' said David as they stood outside, his arm around her waist, 'it's our first house.'

Once they arrived in Lesbos they quickly settled into a routine. David would rise early, around 5 a.m., and leave Sue sleeping while he crept downstairs to write. Around 8 a.m. she would wake and lean out of bed to peer through the gaps between the old floorboards, to see him working in the room

---

* In *A Perfect Spy* Heumann would serve as the model for the character of Axel, the Czech spy to whom Pym betrays all his secrets.

below. Eventually she would shower and dress, and join him downstairs, before heading out to fetch supplies and the local English-language newspaper. He explained what he was writing. 'It's about my dad,' he told her. 'I'm writing about me and my dad.' This was the autobiographical novel that would be published in 1986 under the title *A Perfect Spy*.* 'I've been trying to write about him for years and failing to for even longer,' he said. 'Now I *am* writing about him and it's got a lot to do with a tall and lovely girl.' From now on, he told her, she would be 'my Muse as well as my Recording Angel'.

When Sue eventually read *A Perfect Spy* she would recognise snatches of their conversation in the mouths of his characters. In one part of the story, the central figure, Magnus Pym, is trying to write a novel while on holiday on Lesbos (in fact at Plomari) – though he is with his wife, not his mistress, and his young son, who is a similar age to David's own son Nick at the time.

Each day, when he finished writing, David would go out by himself to telephone his wife from the payphone in the post office – to 'radio base' as he put it. There was always an artificiality about him when he came back from calling home. He called the process 'decompression'. Afterwards they would buy fresh bread and local cheeses and olives and head to the beach for lunch. On their first morning on Lesbos, David had set off shopping for beach clothes. When Sue asked why he hadn't brought any, he looked at her as if she had asked a stupid question. 'I thought it inadvisable to be seen packing any.' In a village shop

---

* At first he wanted to call it *Agent Running in the Field*, a title he would use for another novel published in 2019. His preferred title after that was *The Love Thief*.

he bought two T-shirts and two pairs of swimming trunks, which he would jettison at the end of the holiday. Then he asked the shopkeeper the way to the main beach. Once they were out of sight of the shop, David led Sue in the opposite direction.

One morning David set off for a walk alone, telling her that he would be back in an hour at most. 'You don't mind if I go off for a while, do you, my love?' he asked. 'Just for a walk and to read the paper?' She pointed out that he was carrying yesterday's newspaper, but he assured her that it didn't matter. Later, when she read *A Perfect Spy*, she would find that Pym carries a copy of the previous day's newspaper to signal to watchers that he wants a meeting. This was her first experience of David's method of acting out scenes that he would later write about.

'I'm just a writer, you know,' David remarked one day while they were sitting on the beach. 'I'm happy if people like my stuff.' Of course he didn't mean anything of the kind. When he continued that he had written ten novels – 'it's not nothing' – and she joked that they should have given him the Queen's Award to Industry, he seemed to take her comment seriously. 'They offered me a K this year,'* he confided: 'I turned them down.' He indicated that he had 'turned them down' before. She had begun to appreciate that he was sensitive about his anomalous status: hugely successful commercially, but not awarded the status of a 'literary' writer. Later he told her that she lacked gravitas – apparently a reference to a joke-telling contest in the tavern he had lost the night before. 'I've told Rainer I don't wish to be considered for the Nobel,' he continued in a startling non sequitur. Much later, when she complained that he had no right

---

* i.e. a knighthood.

to make her suffer for his art, she was dumbfounded by his reply: 'Would you have said that to Goethe?'

Over a midday drink in one of the bars that ringed the harbour in Plomari, David told her about his children, and his first wife, Ann. When Sue suggested that Ann might have been the model for Smiley's wife, David contradicted her. 'No, Smiley's Ann isn't *my* Ann,' he said. 'I think *his* Ann may be *you*.' He expatiated on this theme as he gazed out to sea: Sue was his 'dream woman', 'the girl on the beach I can't have'. Sue suggested that he was wrong, that he could have her; but David was insistent. 'No,' he insisted. 'Like this, yes. But no, not now.' He continued staring out to sea. 'You should have come to me earlier,' he went on. 'Before I got myself banged up for life.'

On their last evening David shocked Sue by suggesting that they break it off. 'Shall we say it's over?' he asked. 'Shall we call it the best holiday in the world but say it's over? And just stay friends?' He relented in the face of her vehement protests. 'If we stay together I should have to get out from Hampstead – from the slammer I've made for myself there,' he went on. He warned her that it might take a while. 'You're so wise,' he told her. 'Much more than me. I get such blacks. Such dreadful thoughts.'

The next day they flew back to Athens, where they planned to spend the night in a hotel before leaving for Zurich in the morning. As they waited by the carousel for their bags, David stiffened. 'Don't touch me!' he whispered. 'It's Steve and the whole fucking crew.' A group was waiting by another carousel, and one of them, a young man who was obviously David's son, was peering in their direction. Suddenly cold, David commanded her to wait while he walked over to talk to them. A few minutes later he returned and loaded their bags onto a trolley, treating her as if she were someone he had just chanced to meet, and a nuisance at that. He informed her that he had arranged to have supper with the crew. Though they were heading for the same hotel, he insisted on travelling in separate taxis.

Back in London, Sue received a letter from David to say that he was 'progressing in his efforts to extricate himself from his domestic situation'. He planned to go down to Cornwall over half-term to 'hammer something out down there'. Sue was disconcerted. She was still young and not ready for a life-changing commitment; she was more than happy just to be his mistress.

Perhaps to make amends for the excruciating scene at the airport, David took Sue to lunch at Odin's on Devonshire Street in Marylebone, then very much a place to see and be seen. She noted the date: the day before his fifty-second birthday. After they had ordered, he remarked that Harold Pinter was seated at his usual table; she realised later that David had taken her there because he had expected to see the famous playwright and wanted to show off his young and attractive girlfriend. Over lunch he told Sue that his sister Charlotte wanted to meet her. She was puzzled: only a few days before he'd refused to acknowledge her in front of one member of his family, and now he wanted to introduce her to another. Who was allowed to know about her existence, and who wasn't? More important, he was buying a flat. 'I've told my chief scout in these matters that I want a pad where I can write and get away from my family to entertain my bird.' He wanted a place far enough from Hampstead to create some space, but close enough that he could get back there in a hurry if required; the agent thought that he had found somewhere suitable. While she was still digesting this news David gave her what he called a 'birthday present' (though it was his birthday, not hers): an eighteenth-century cage-link gold necklace, secured by a gauntleted hand, set with turquoise. 'It's to say hold on, my darling,' he explained. 'It's not going to be easy and it's not going to be quick,' he continued. 'But I'm heading for the shore.'

Ten days later, on a Saturday morning towards the end of October, Sue boarded a train bound for Cornwall. To please David she had replaced her spectacles with contact lenses. He picked her up in the car from the station in Penzance (the end of the line). Half-term was nearly over, and Sue deduced that Jane and their son Nick had left that same morning. She wondered what they had 'hammered out' together. The countryside seemed to her desolate. As they arrived at St Buryan, the nearest village to the house, David mentioned that 'Peckinpah filmed *Straw Dogs* here'. When they arrived at Tregiffian, David proudly showed her around and Sue made all the right noises, though she was a city girl at heart and didn't see the appeal of living in such a bleak place. It seemed to her a form of exile – but from what? After a meal in front of a blazing log fire, he asked her if she'd been calling the house. At first she didn't understand what he meant, because she didn't know the Tregiffian telephone number. 'Not here, Hampstead,' he explained. 'Jane's been getting calls. Someone ringing and not speaking when she picks up. She lives in terror of kidnappers.' Apparently Jane had raised the alarm when she had spotted wires hanging underneath the car and a smashed tail light. The police had cordoned off the area while the Bomb Squad had checked it out. Was this perhaps a sign of self-importance, or paranoia?*

---

* In the 1970s and 1980s several bombs planted by the Provisional IRA targeted individuals' homes. At least once a passer-by was killed in the resulting explosion.

The next day he took her to lunch at Sancreed House with John Miller and his partner Michael Truscott. Miller, David had told her, was his best friend. The lunch seemed to Sue a pleasant occasion, though somehow artificial: she felt as if they were on show, like actors putting on a performance. At the end of the meal David refused coffee, saying that he had some calls to make at home. As he saw them to the door Miller murmured to Sue, 'David always has to have a reason for leaving.'

Back at the house, they set out on a walk along the coastal footpath. After a while she asked him how the conversations over half-term had gone. A chill descended. 'We talked,' he said after a long interval, and spoke no more until they were back at the house, except to shout commands to the two dogs. She felt as if she had somehow offended him by asking about what he had told her he would do. 'I don't need you here, you know,' he said, as they shed their waxed jackets, 'if you're going to be moody.'

The tension continued for several days. As always they continued to have sex, but like strangers; there was no communication between them. David moaned and mumbled in his sleep. He took her to see Derek Tangye, whom she loathed, especially when he groped her under the kitchen table.

One afternoon George Greenfield arrived at Tregiffian with his girlfriend,* bringing with them a welcome sense of normality. The two women, both mistresses to married men, formed an instant and lasting bond. But Sue still felt that her visit to Cornwall had been a failure. The next morning she took the train back to London, yet again feeling 'lost and confused'.

---

* Unidentified to protect her privacy. In her book Sue gave her the pseudonym 'Gigi'.

A few days after her return she received an unrepentant letter from David, in which he concluded by saying that he didn't like 'being pushed around'. He asked her to write back, *poste restante* Hampstead.*

Over the weeks that followed they managed to see each other occasionally, but often in only snatched meetings because of other claims on his time, from accountants, lawyers, film people, builders, and his family. To her, his busy schedule resembled a plate-spinning routine, though why he needed to keep so many plates in the air at once remained a mystery. His constant complaint was that he was being taken away from his new book. He had by this time adopted more of his father's expressions, such as 'a full and frank exchange of views', a euphemism for sex. He already had his own vernacular, a kind of facetious slumming: referring to the booksellers Waterstone's as 'Wasserstein's' (a literal translation into German), for example, or his publishers Hodder & Stoughton as 'Odders and Sodders'. He began to refer to her as 'Our Sue'. Several characters in his books – usually the more dislikeable ones – speak in what he dubbed 'Belgravia cockney'.†

She returned to Cornwall about a month later. This time the atmosphere was more relaxed. 'Do you ski?' he asked one day, when he had been telling her about his chalet in Wengen. 'You're no use to me if you don't ski. We could go there all the time if you did.' He gave her an early Christmas present of a gold pendant, set with a delicate coral and lapis lazuli carving of Venus rising from the sea. Afterwards they travelled back to

---

* i.e. kept at the post office to await collection.

† 'Belgravia cockney, thought Guillam: the last stage of linguistic collapse.' (*The Honourable Schoolboy*, p. 190.)

London together by train. As they sat opposite each other in the first-class carriage, David proposed that she should help him find out about his father Ronnie, by researching his past: his business schemes, his convictions for fraud, his 'court' of criminal associates, his attempt to stand for parliament to avoid military service, his involvement with sports and showbiz celebrities, even the racehorses he owned. 'It might be fun and the pay will be excellent, though one of the terms of your contract will be that you are required to engage in frequent bouts of intensely inventive sex with your employer.' Though he did not say this explicitly, employing her as a researcher would provide a form of cover for their meetings. He promised her a credit in his book. She promised to think about it and let him know.

Back in London, David took Sue to dinner with his sister. After saying hello, Charlotte spoke barely another word to her the whole evening, and instead talked intently to her brother over the dining-room table. Sue felt as if she might as well not have been there. It occurred to her that any observer of the scene would assume Charlotte to have been David's girlfriend, not her. She was bemused when he telephoned her the next evening to say how much his sister had liked her.

David maintained 'radio silence' over Christmas and New Year, but one afternoon in early January he took her to see his new flat in St John's Wood. Though it wasn't yet ready to be occupied, he was excited to show it to her. It was on the top floor of the building, up three flights of stairs. 'You're the only one I'm ever going to let in here,' he declared. When Sue told him that she was going to America for ten days to see some old friends, David grudgingly awarded her 'a lot of Brownie points' for arranging a holiday on her own. Only half-jokingly, he suggested that she might be going to meet her other lover, 'that much older fellow', with 'nothing like' his staying power.

Immediately on her return, while she was still jet-lagged from her transatlantic flight, he whisked her off to Zurich, where they stayed at The Dolder Grand, a five-star hotel in a magnificent position, with a terrace offering a panorama of the Alps across Lake Zurich. In their bedroom she presented him with her ski pass, gift-wrapped in tissue paper and wrapped in ribbon: evidence that, while on holiday in New Hampshire, she had learned to ski as a present to him, so that she could accompany him in future. He seemed delighted, though as things turned out he never took her to the chalet in Wengen, and they would never go skiing together.

By the time Sue next visited the St John's Wood flat, it was furnished and ready for occupation. David had installed a front door of heavy steel, which he pronounced bulletproof.* Naturally he had installed a peephole, so that he could see who was at the door before opening it. While they were lying in bed together, he read her pages from the book he was working on, and she observed that his satisfaction after reading his own work was much the same as after sex. 'I'm finally writing the book I want to be buried with,' he told her.†

They met often, but almost never without his cancelling or rearranging one or two dates beforehand, the disappointments allayed by big bouquets of flowers, and her expectations raised by flattery and a steady flow of treats. Even when she wasn't with

---

* According to the man who installed it, this description is 'bollocks'.
† Presumably meant metaphorically, though perhaps also a reference to the notebook of Rossetti's poems that the poet had interred with his wife's coffin. David was cremated at his own wish.

him, she still felt under his control. After a while he gave her a set of keys to the flat, but this didn't mean that he trusted her entirely. He warned her that he would know if she had taken another lover there; and tested her by leaving his papers face down on the table, carefully aligned so that he could tell whether they had been examined while he was out. But in *A Perfect Spy* he has Magnus Pym do the same while he is in Greece with his wife, so perhaps this was just another rehearsal.

Near the flat they discovered a Chinese restaurant. 'No one knows us here,' David said with a sigh of relief, as they sat contemplating the menu one lunchtime. 'It feels like sanctuary at last.' He scanned the room above the menu. '*Christ – it's Freddie!*' he whispered. The thriller writer Frederick Forsyth had just entered with his wife. A moment later a voice boomed across the restaurant. '*Good Lord!* David, old man, we meet *at last*!' Apparently the Forsyths lived nearby. After the meal they were invited back to their house for a drink. When David accepted a brandy, Forsyth turned to Sue. 'What about you, Jane?' he asked.

'I've been thinking,' David said to her one day, as he escorted her down St John's Wood High Street towards the Tube station. 'Would a girl like a little cottage in Cornwall so as to be handy for her lover? And maybe a starter-kit car to go with it – a *deux chevaux*,* perhaps, and driving lessons to go with it?' She resisted this offer.

A conversation between the two of them about writers he admired led her to confess that she had no German. 'Ah well,' he replied, 'you're no use to me if you don't speak German.'

---

* A Citroën 2CV (two steam horsepower), a small, inexpensive car based on a design introduced in 1948.

For Sue this was another challenge, so without his knowledge she enrolled on a four-week intensive course in German at the Goethe-Institut in South Kensington. David was 'thrilled' when, halfway through the course, she told him about it. In bed afterwards he spoke to her in German.

Sue had agreed to David's proposal that she investigate his father's life. She proved an assiduous researcher, and colourful material soon began to accumulate. David was delighted with each new find, her discoveries feeding his inventions. As her research progressed, David suggested that she might 'go the whole hog' and write his father's biography. It was a daunting proposition for someone so young and inexperienced; but the more she thought about it, the more confident she became.

At some point she decided that the time had come for them to let Graham Goodwin, her boss at the recording studio, into their secret. The three of them lunched together at the same Soho trattoria where she and David had gone when they had first met. It made Sue happy to be there together with two of her favourite men, both of whom she loved, and both of whom in their different ways loved her too. In the taxi up to St John's Wood afterwards her happiness bubbled over. She was dismayed when David responded by disparaging the other man.* 'The thing about Graham, one always feels, is that there's somehow less to him than the sum of his parts.' She railed at him, furious

---

* Much later she discovered that David had disparaged her to George Greenfield and his girlfriend, after they had met at Tregiffian. On the evening after she left, Greenfield had remarked that she self-evidently had a good mind. 'Oh, come off it, George,' David had countered; 'she only got a 2:1.' This remark infuriated her.

that he should speak so dismissively about her great friend. It occurred to her that he surrounded himself with sycophants, very few of whom ever dared to contradict him.

On the morning of Sue's birthday he gave her a gold wristwatch, with a card reading 'For time present and time past and time forever'. Then Greenfield and his girlfriend arrived at the flat, bearing a bottle of Dom Pérignon. They embraced, and laughed, and talked excitably, and afterwards David took the three of them for an opulent lunch at The Connaught. That night she accompanied him in a taxi to Paddington, to see him off on the midnight sleeper to Penzance. For Sue it seemed a perfect day.

It came as a shock to her when, a couple of days later, he telephoned her from Tregiffian to say that he wanted to end their relationship. 'I can't go on,' he told her, and rang off. Stunned, she reacted by rushing to Paddington and catching the next available train down to Cornwall. Many tears and much talking and walking followed. The next day they drove back to London together, stopping for a pub lunch on the way.

David had proposed three weeks of 'radio silence', but almost immediately reneged on his resolution. Before the three weeks had elapsed they were in Vienna, supposedly to scout out locations for *A Perfect Spy*: Magnus Pym is deputy head of station there. On their first morning in the city David led her to 'some serious shops' and proceeded to spend some serious money on clothes for her. Then they travelled on to Munich, where David was to receive an award. Sue remained at the hotel while he attended the ceremony. She switched on the television in their hotel room, to find that the ceremony was being broadcast live; it felt as if every channel was covering David in some form or other. When he returned to the hotel later that evening, she commented on how extensive the coverage had been. 'Yes, I know,' he said. 'The Krauts love me.' A further demonstration of his status in Germany came when he accompanied her to a photography exhibition at the Goethe-Institut. The staff all stopped what they were doing to stare at him, and the Director himself appeared to greet the Great Man, who was respectfully invited to sign the visitors' book.

In the middle of May, Sue accepted David's invitation to spend a few days with him in Cornwall. On their first morning, while they were chatting over coffee, the telephone rang. From David's tone of 'pained endurance' she deduced that the caller was Jane, and tactfully absented herself. She was sitting on the sofa in another room when David stormed in a few minutes later. He leaped on top of her, pinning her down, his forearm against her throat. 'You did that *deliberately*, didn't you?' he seethed. She had no clue what he was talking about. 'She heard you!' he went on. '"You've got somebody *with* you," she said. "I can hear her *heels* on the flagstones—"'

Sue protested that she had just been trying to give him some privacy. He stared down at her. 'Your credibility hangs by a *thread*,' he said eventually, and relaxed his hold. The next morning, as she ascended the stairs with a cup of coffee, she found him removing her belongings from the marital bedroom, in preparation for the arrival of his accountant, to whom she was introduced as his researcher. Sue left the next morning, resolved never to return to Tregiffian again.

The summer of 1984 was miserable. Sue continued to see David often, but she wearied of 'the constant threnody about the book, how everything and everyone was taking him away from it, including the time he spent with me. There were unceasing complaints about his wife, his family and whomever else he felt encumbered by, which appeared to be everybody.' His letters were sometimes loving and encouraging, sometimes nasty and accusatory. She found herself moaning about how he treated her; she was humiliated to have allowed herself to become reduced to such a state. She tried everything she could think of to put things right. On one occasion she turned up at the flat wearing nothing but a Burberry raincoat and high heels.

'You're a rich man's mistress now,' Graham Goodwin told her, as they sat together watching a men's singles match on the Centre Court at Wimbledon. 'Them's the rules of the game.'

Sue protested that she had never wanted to be anything other than David's mistress. He was the one who insisted that he had to get out of his marriage, who made promises that he went on to break, and set deadlines that he didn't keep.

Goodwin insisted that David was never going to leave his wife. When Sue asked why, if that was so, he kept saying that he wanted to leave, Goodwin argued that it was the tension that he liked – the very thing that was making her so miserable.

'I thought you liked him,' Sue said plaintively.

'I do, honey – I think he's great. But then, I ain't sleeping with him, am I?'

In early July, Sue made an unannounced visit to David's flat. When she started to tell him that she had decided to go ahead with Ronnie's biography, he cut her off: he didn't think that was a good idea anymore. For her to write the book seemed to him loaded with perils. Sue was almost hysterical with frustration. She quickly dressed and left.

In a subsequent letter, David asked her forgiveness for his 'zig-zagging'. He felt that everything he did was a betrayal of some sort. He also felt that he must concentrate on the novel he was writing. He suggested the beginning of October as a deadline for deciding what to do about the future. Meanwhile, he said, he intended to 'go hellbent' for the book. By now he was using Ronnie's vernacular almost compulsively, for example speaking of slipping out for a 'small wet'.

Later in the summer David telephoned to say that he planned to come to London for a few days. Would she meet him at the flat? She agreed, and for a short while she was happy again. But when the self-imposed decision date came around, David was not ready to decide, as quickly became clear during another rendezvous at the flat. How could he possibly be held to a deadline? He didn't need anyone upsetting his equilibrium at this late stage of the book. Once this was finished, he meant to move out, for weekdays to begin with – perhaps to Oxford, perhaps to Berlin. Understandably frustrated, Sue walked out. When she reached home she gathered up all the jewellery he had ever given her and sent it back to him by courier.

'Wait until the spring,' he urged her. 'Then I'll have done the book and we can sort ourselves out ...' He bought her an early Christmas present, an antique eternity ring in platinum, set with diamonds. 'From your eternal lover,' he said, as he attempted, unsuccessfully, to slide it onto her finger: 'For the eternity of pain I've caused you and the eternal future we may or may not have.'

In mid-December he took her back to Zurich for a short stay at The Dolder Grand. When they arrived the light was fading, and the air was crisp and cold. They took a taxi to the old town and wandered along the lanes until they found an inviting *bier-keller* with a blazing log fire. They sat holding hands at a corner table, hardly talking, content just to watch and listen. The next morning she woke early, to find him lying motionless beside her, staring at the ceiling. She imagined that he must have lain awake like this for hours. 'You have to go back,' he said, without looking at her. 'I can't be this happy.'

Sue was in despair. She felt as if she had nothing left to give. Somehow they struggled on until the following summer, when she felt able to break it off.

'I think you were very lucky to have the strength to get out when you did, before he used you up completely,' Greenfield's girlfriend told her. According to George, Jane had been 'hoovered up' since her marriage. His private nickname for David was 'the monster'.

A Perfect Spy was published in the spring of 1986. Three months earlier Sue had received a letter from David, apologising for the fact that he had not acknowledged her research help in the novel as he had promised. He had been advised that this might undermine the book's claim to be a work of fiction and could possibly invite legal action from anyone who might consider themselves to have been defamed. Furious, she posted a typed letter to his home address, which she hoped Jane would open and read before he saw it, demanding that he keep his word. In due course she received a typed reply, with a commitment that the acknowledgement would appear in later editions of the book, as indeed it did. He signed his letter 'Yours sincerely'.

FIVE

An epistolary romance

In the autumn of 1993 David received a fan letter from a reader in Los Angeles, who had been prompted to read *The Night Manager* after seeing him talking about it on television. She deplored the fact that such a serious novel should be stocked in the 'mystery' section of the bookstores. In his reply, he thanked her for writing 'so interestingly ... I was very touched by all you had to say, and fascinated by many of your insights.' She wrote again, and a correspondence began that would last more than two years. Because they lived so far apart, their relationship was almost entirely epistolary, but it quickly became intimate. Though David's first letter was typed, all his subsequent letters were handwritten, most of them early in the morning, or late at night, often with a glass of whisky at his side. What she had written had piqued his interest and made him want to continue the contact. 'You write a lovely letter,' he told her. 'I really enjoy knowing you. Are you safe? Who are you?'

She was Susan Anderson, a museum curator and published poet with ambitions to write fiction herself, successful in her career but discontented in her marriage and ready for an adventure. I was unaware of her existence until I came across two

letters David wrote to her in the collection edited by his son
Tim and published in 2022. I made contact with her by email,
and subsequently we had several long conversations via Zoom. It
cannot have been easy for her to discuss her intimate past with a
complete stranger, and I was impressed by her frankness, articu-
lacy and insight.

She told me that she had never before read John le Carré
when she happened to catch the episode of *The Charlie Rose
Show* in which David was interviewed for an hour, talking both
about *The Night Manager* (then recently published) and more
generally about what he would write now that the Cold War
was over. By this time in his early sixties, he looked healthy and
relaxed, wearing an open-necked denim shirt which contrasted
with the suit worn by his interviewer. As always he spoke flu-
ently and eloquently, in a soft, mellifluous voice. To Susan he
appeared both vital and handsome. She had been delighted by
the progressive views he expressed, especially his disparagement
of empire.

Though normally snooty about 'thrillers', Susan had been
persuaded to buy his book, and had read it on a trip to the
Caribbean, where much of the action of the novel was set. By the
time she returned, she was 'a bit obsessed'. She had just turned
forty, which seemed to her a landmark in her life. She longed
to be a mature, desired woman, 'like Jeanne Moreau: no longer
girlish, but ripe, alluring, and wise', as she put it. Her letters have
not survived, but she kept all of his, which makes it possible to
trace the history of their relationship in detail. They show how
tightly his work and his emotional life were intertwined; and
how much his composure depended on his ability to write.

Most of David's letters to Susan are quite long, often six or

DAVID CORNWELL

14th October 1993

Ms. Susan Anderson,

Dear Susan Anderson,

Thank you so much for your letter of the 24th September. Forgive this typed letter in reply. I was very touched by all you had to say, and fascinated by many of your insights. You mustn't worry too much when you find me in the shelves marked 'Mysteries'. I have had the great good fortune to be read by all sorts of readers, and if my books are more accessible to them by being described as 'Thrillers' or 'Mysteries', that is a very small price to pay for such a splendid readership.

I will confess to you that I absolutely detest appearing on television, or indeed, appearing in public at all. One of these days somebody will string together an analysis of how self-contradictory my interviews have been in the aggregate. And the reason is that I am alternately bored and scared by the whole process. Meanwhile, I have a wonderful life in Cornwall, in absolute seclusion, and at sixty-two seem to have hit one of the best writing periods of my life.

Thank you again for writing so interestingly. And thank you for your kind words.

Yours sincerely,

DAVID CORNWELL

Letter to Susan Anderson, a response to a fan letter written after she had seen him interviewed on the *Charlie Rose* TV talkshow.

seven pages in extent. He wrote to her on average once every three weeks, sometimes more frequently, sometimes less. At least one of his early letters was put aside unfinished and resumed several weeks later. In them he told her about his work, his life in Cornwall, and aspects of his past that helped to explain why he was the way he was. 'I <u>like</u> talking to you, & you're a great talker back, and your letters are in my memory locked, & you alone have the key to them,'* he wrote in his third letter, dated 7 February 1994; and he made 'one serious request', that she would give him the same assurance. 'Sometimes just writing to you unlocks me, like writing to my muse ... But sooner or later we must peek through the keyhole in the confession box, & find out who we are, I suppose ...'

In his early letters he seemed to have been probing the boundaries of their relations, testing the limits of what was acceptable. 'I don't want to ask you whether you're married, though I sense that you are,' he continued: 'actually I don't want to ask you anything ordinary at all, whether you are sixty or thirty or long or short or white or black ... I want to ask you for a photograph, but that would be too like casting.' (Soon afterwards she would send him a photo, revealing that she was, as perhaps he suspected, a woman of colour, with luxuriant curling dark hair.)

In the same letter he confessed that on a recent brief visit to Los Angeles to meet the director Sydney Pollack, to discuss making a movie of *The Night Manager*, he had contemplated telephoning to ask her out to dinner – 'but then I fretted and thought I might embarrass you – or something, I don't know,

---

* *Hamlet*, Act 1, Scene 3. Ophelia says to her brother, "Tis in my memory locked, And you yourself shall keep the key of it.'

4

until the 4 a.m. screams begin,
and we've all had them since 30,
which seems to be the age where
death starts roosting on your roof.
I'm still fine. And the art of it
all is to go on being fine for as
long as you can. The best bit of
my life was somewhere in the late
forties to the late sixties, I think.
I want to die a child. There's no
other way to live. You write a
lovely letter. I really enjoy knowing
you. Are you safe? Who are you?
Happy Christmas / New Year, happy you.
Best — David

Extract from a letter to Susan Anderson, begun on
18 November and completed on 13 December 1993.

& maybe that there just <u>wasn't</u> the space, & maybe writing is what we like better. Does that feel like a great betrayal or a great relief?'

'Yours was a <u>very</u> sexy letter,' he added in a postscript, and asked her to write in future to a different address, 'because it's more private for me': c/o John Miller at Sancreed House. 'That's my dead letter box for really <u>disgraceful</u> correspondence.' He instructed her that letters to him should be sealed inside an envelope addressed to Miller.

This method of communication incurred delays, and the intervals between posting a letter to the other side of the world and receiving a response led to several misunderstandings. To mitigate this danger he began to use an express postal service called Swiftair, though this necessitated a visit to the post office each time he wanted to communicate with her. He was reluctant to talk on the telephone 'because (1) I hate the phone and (2) something changes – I need to see you, touch you, once I have heard your voice ... the phone will definitely unsettle both of us'.

His letters occasionally mentioned Jane, but only in passing. 'It's no good talking to each other about our marriages,' he wrote. Instead he provided a running commentary on the progress of his writing. On a good day the words streamed from his pen. 'I've reached a point now, 300 pp. in, where I can write economically, almost first time okay, because at this stage if you don't know what you're doing you better shoot yourself.' On a bad day it was almost the opposite: 'You look at your own words so many times you learn to hate them, which is quite unfair; and each time you look you have to coax yourself into some kind of enthusiasm or you're dead in the bathtub ...'

In these early letters he circled around the question of whether they should continue as strangers writing secret letters to each other, or whether they should risk meeting. At this stage, and for some time after, Susan had no real intention of starting an affair. For her, the correspondence was an escapist fantasy, a delightful change from routine reality; but he kept pushing for them to take things further. His mounting excitement is palpable on the page, as his letters became more erotic and more explicit.

Quite soon he was fantasising on paper about what might happen when they were together. The very act of writing was like the act of love. After posting a long letter, he 'felt a great sense of loss. It was as if we had made love, & at once you had jumped out of bed to clean your teeth.' Again he raised the possibility of an encounter.

> I don't want to meet you in England but there's the rest of Europe and there are other bits of America. It just needs working out ... I relish you as the most beautiful woman in the world. You stand somewhere between the end of a garden and the sea, emerging from a large oyster shell, with only your black hair for chastity ...

This image must have stimulated him, because he returned to it a month later. 'I need more of you. I am beginning to write something wonderful. Stay on your oyster shell. Wear nothing.'

His next letter expressed the fear that he had gone too far. 'Dearest You,' he wrote,

> I nearly died when I didn't hear from you, I thought I had been too bold, too broad, too presumptuous ... Then yesterday I went to Sancreed like a boy, trembling & sick, and found your

letters ... and I brought the letters home & read them in my workroom and could have walked on the sea although there was a Force Six gale coming off the Atlantic.

Almost in the same breath, however, he warned that he would not be able to join her at a writers' retreat in the Blue Ridge Mountains, where she had proposed that they might stay a while and write their novels together. This did not suit his method of working, which excluded all distraction. For the next few months he would be preoccupied with his new novel,* including a planned visit to the Caucasus, where Chechen rebels were fighting a war of independence against Russian rule, and where the climax of the action was set. 'And so we'll have to burn alone for a while longer, but I'm not sure that's the worst thing in the world either, it means we can get a lot of talking done, and live a little longer in this clean air, and hold hands from a distance while we write our books.' He warned her that 'for chunks of this time I'll be off the air'.

Even so, when he didn't hear from her for a month he became anxious, worrying that he had put her off, that it was over, and that she didn't want to write any more. He wrote to her as if their relationship had ended, before they had even met. 'You got too deep inside me somehow,' he lamented: 'I began to depend on you, on writing to you, and hearing from you.' But the day after he had sent this, he received a reassuring letter from her, explaining why she had not written: in the remote Blue Ridge Mountains she had been unable to get to a post office. 'You kiss

---

* Provisionally entitled *The Passion of His Time*, but eventually published as *Our Game*.

my letters; I kiss yours,' he wrote happily: 'by whatever strange route, I love you, and am joined to you, and that's the mystery of it.' He apologised for 'the pain I had inadvertently caused you'. Once again he urged her to keep his letters private. 'Susan, concerning my insecurities: these letters that you kiss, and which as time goes by contain my closest secrets, or may ... I care terribly that they should <u>never</u> see the light of day.'*

In David's mind, consummation of their passion and the completion of his book were one, almost simultaneous. It seemed to him that

> once I have the whole book, I should take it on safari, read it in different lights, moods, places, sharpen it, remove all adverbs and find the right verbs instead, and make love to you. And that our lovemaking should have a carefully chosen context – like the mountains where you were, or a quiet French village, or a Greek island, or a motel in Detroit (perhaps not) – somewhere that is safe, our own place entirely, and beautiful and walkable, and where we can close the door and resolve the vexed question of where to sit, what on, and which way round ...

Several of his letters expressed the fear that he was impotent, and in one he explicitly identified the act of writing with the act of love.

---

* When, more than twenty years later, she decided to dispose of the letters, the agent she used offered David the chance to buy them; and when he did not take this up, she felt free to offer them elsewhere. David sent her a message saying that he wanted to talk to her, but she declined, a decision she now regrets.

One day I'm ~~importa~~ (Freudian mis-spelling) impotent, the next erect again, whole pages whizzed off, look at me, I can take on the entire front row of the chorus, next day flop again, useless; I can't even remember what it was like before. It was always about energy, courage, libido, fear, laughter – it was always a first book every time, there's no such thing as a pro, not really. Just an industrious, persistent, stubborn first timer ...

He sent her a lock of his hair as a keepsake. 'Please,' he begged her, 'when we are finally face to face on some blessed pillow, let's remember how long we have been lovers.'

Of course they had not been lovers at all: by the end of August they had been corresponding for almost a year, and still had yet to meet. The action remained on the page. 'My guess is that we'll still make it this year somehow somewhere,' he wrote, 'but I have you, & you have me, & the wonder of you is, you let me breathe & write & fly first.' He thanked her for being his 'secret sharer' through the writing of the second half of the book. As so many times before, he anticipated the rapture of their eventual meeting. 'I'm <u>sure</u> I'm impotent but I suspect you can repair that, and I feel very protective of you at this minute, & just want to give you a great big hug.'

Ten days later he wrote again, in a cautious response to a suggestion of hers. 'A friend's house in Cape Cod in October sounds seriously inviting. I wld be so much happier if we cd meet this autumn somehow.' But only a couple of weeks afterwards he was backpedalling.

My darling, late October is in the balance, to say the least. Knopf want to publish in early spring, galleys by the end of November. They like it v much and have paid the required ransome [*sic*] for it but I have to get at it, as I always do as soon as I've sent it out, & re-do a lot of stuff … Darling, I'm going to do my best, but steel yourself for my <u>not</u> making it, as I must steel <u>myself</u>, unless I can get a huge spurt on & satisfy myself, not them, they're easier …

When it seemed likely that he might have to undertake the dangerous trip to the Caucasus, Susan had sent him a St Christopher's medal on a chain, to carry with him and keep him safe. On her birthday in September he sent her a turquoise and gold necklace, addressed to 'My beloved secret sharer, with thanks & love,' and signed 'Soon, D.'

Early in October he began a letter, 'Dearest Susan, listen carefully …' He would be coming to New York for the week beginning 20 October, to work with 'the Knopfniks' on the American edition of the book; and once he was free of commitments, he could join her in Cape Cod for the weekend. It was not much, far less than he had often proposed, but she agreed nonetheless. After several telephone conversations in which she was nervous and he reassured her, he arrived unexpectedly early on the Friday evening, bearing champagne, foie gras, and a typescript of his novel, which he presented to her.

It was extraordinary to be in each other's company at last, after more than a year of corresponding. It seemed to them both miraculous that they had met and fallen in love just through writing to each other, and that this had been enough to sustain them for so long. 'This is the kind of thing that makes you believe in God,' said David. The first full day together was spent giddily in bed, and they didn't get dressed until the evening, when they went out to dine in a local restaurant.

The next day David's mood was sombre. While Susan was sitting on his lap, he told her about seeing young boys with guns who had danced in a circle around Yasser Arafat, leader of the Palestinian Liberation Organization. Susan was horrified: though she understood children's participation in the intifada, she felt strongly that to train them as combatants was wrong. 'You're such an <u>American</u>,' David remarked disdainfully.

But this was a sour note in an otherwise happy encounter. A taxi arrived at dawn on the Monday morning to take him back to New York. It waited while they made their goodbyes, its engine running, in a little copse of pine trees. After he left, Susan, still in her flimsy nightdress, collapsed sobbing to the floor; then, to her surprise, he came back, and grabbed her in a fierce embrace. Though he was leaving, he promised, he wasn't going anywhere. She spent the rest of her retreat working energetically on her manuscript.

Afterwards he wrote her a long, 'special' letter – full of news about the book. The morning after his return to London, he had 'hurled myself at the rewrite,' responding to his American editor's comments* – 'it's <u>miles</u> better'. Much of the credit he gave to Susan. 'I can't see or think anything without referring it to you ...' He gave her an address to write to in London: c/o Rex Cowan, a lawyer turned swashbuckling shipwreck-finder, who lived nearby in Hampstead and had a holiday home in Cornwall.

'I think of you constantly,' he wrote after his return to Cornwall, 'at the closest quarters, in the most abstract ways, as an ally always to be trusted and never shocked, as <u>a person beyond</u>

---

* His American editor was now 'Sonny' Mehta, editor-in-chief at Knopf since 1987.

London 1st Nov 94

My darling,

It had to be a special letter, nothing hasty, nothing on the run. I got back on Monday night and by Tues am at 5.0 I had hurled myself at the rewrite. The finished work went off to Sonny yesterday & he'll call me tomorrow when he's read it, but I'm not worried — it's _miles_ better, it's what he painted in the air, with all sorts of other elements thrown in — the vividness and exhilaration & renewal that I brought back with me, more anger, more externalisation of feeling, a _lot_ of bad language suddenly, more highs & lows — a total immersion of a rewrite, and you in large part to thank for it. I can't see or think anything without referring it to you, even if you'd reject it on the grounds of age, irrelevance, or because you are too busy making love to

The first page of a letter written to Susan Anderson after their one and, as it turned out, only meeting.

reproach ...' He promised to write again very soon: 'but don't fret when there are pauses.' Back in London again, he admitted to feeling stale:

> I pretty much signed off on [the book] last night when I synthesized the UK and US edited tss, copying corrections from one to the other, then sending them off by courier. The effect of pre-publication bureaucracy is always the same on me. It's like – I imagine – waking up in the whorehouse with a hangover and no sexual appetite; you just want to creep away and find a new life, because the old one's suddenly so grimey [*sic*] and stale.

David outlined plans for a play, set in Vienna before the First World War, but it seemed that his heart was not in it. 'I've never written this sort of stuff ...' He suspected that the cure for his malaise 'lies too far away from me at present, in California I suppose, on one side of a big bed I'm not in & should be ...'

In a further letter, written on 16 December 1994, he offered the possibility of a meeting in mid-March: he might need to fly to Los Angeles then, and could be free to go somewhere with Susan afterwards. Perhaps conscious that these were meagre rations, he praised her forbearance. 'Do you know one reason more why I love you?' he asked. 'Apart from the fact that you & I share some quite rare psycho-physical-sexual wavelength? – You don't beg me to phone you, get cross when I go off the air, you actually do trust me, let me be ...'

Before Christmas she had sent him her own novel, and on 2 January he wrote to tell her that he had just finished reading it. He had been 'deeply impressed and moved. You write beauti-fully ...' He offered his congratulations. 'The joy to me is how much of you is there ...' For all his enthusing, it was clear to Susan that he felt awkward about recommending her to his publisher. Subsequently he made a half-hearted offer to do so, but only under the pretence that she had sent it to him as a stranger.

In a letter dated 17 January he mentioned that Jane had not been at all well. 'I took her to London and Zürich for tests and the results are not terrible but not particularly reassuring either, and I suppose I went into a sort of withdrawal myself ...' Towards the end of the same letter he added, 'so we may have to remain long-distance lovers for longer than I had hoped ...' The following month he again mentioned Jane's illness, telling Susan, 'I can't think of much else,' and that he planned to take his wife 'to one of those White Bastards holiday camps in the Caribbean' for three to four weeks. He warned her that 'You may have to wait a few weeks till you hear from me, but you will, my darling,' and asked her to have faith in him. 'I can't come to you yet, there is too much to worry about here,' he wrote on 7 March, and begged her to 'wait a little longer please, it's going to be a good year, but I have King Richard's monkey on my back* and have to wait a little while before I fling it off again'.

As publication of his novel, now entitled *Our Game*, approached, he sank into melancholy:

> Some sort of private dismay & confusion that I expect always attends publication, but which this time seems deeper & darker, and the sense that I have given another chunk of myself

---

* Perhaps a reference to the Chinese tale of the Monkey King, introduced to the English-speaking world in the nineteenth century by the missionary Timothy Richard, and the origin of the expression 'to have a monkey on one's back'.

away & there aren't too many chunks left, a sense of failure being constantly visible to me – not failure against success, but failure against aspiration, which is the real killer.

She was alarmed by his evident distress and did what she could to cheer and encourage him. In a later letter he would acknowledge her support, 'and the timely kicks in the arse'.

The melancholy deepened into what seems to have been some kind of breakdown,* perhaps precipitated by a witty but malicious review of *Our Game* in the *New Yorker* by John Updike.†
On 23 March, David wrote to Susan from Cornwall:

It's been a weird, scary, silly time. I ran out of the house in London 2 weeks ago and forgot where to go or what I was up to and simply caught a train down here. I slept a bit & had no will to move & now I'm on strange medication and goof about like a happy ghost, except that the local bleeder says I am having a 5-star depression. I don't think <u>that</u> had much to do with it, depression I mean. It was more like a malfunctioning of the bits between the brain & the body, and some kind of secret rage ...

---

* Around this time David was in contact with the actor Stephen Fry, who was also suffering a psychological crisis, and in hiding after suffering stage fright in a production of Simon Gray's play *Cell Mates*. There was intense press interest in his whereabouts, and speculation that he might do himself harm.

† Updike bracketed le Carré with Robert Ludlum, Tom Clancy and Frederick Forsyth, as authors of thrillers 'read on aeroplanes by men in business suits – or rather, in business trousers, with their jackets nicely folded in the overhead rack, and their neckties loosened away from their shirt collars an artful inch'.

He resisted the notion that his breakdown had been related to the publication of *Our Game*; it was 'some other gremlin, some kind of deep gnawing rage or despair that I'd rather not look in the eye ...'

> It never really happened to me like this before. It was like trying to speak and not being able, so you try harder, see yourself disintegrate in your imagination, but meanwhile you're immensely polite to everyone ... I'm sure I'll be all right. But I <u>was</u> scared. You are so lovely to tell me I can do things in the future, great things. I want this one great novel. I haven't really hit it (my form) since A Perfect Spy, & perhaps that's the knowledge that scares ...

A month later he wrote to Susan again, to tell her that he was getting better: 'I'm waking up slowly, just give me time.' It was now six months since their rapturous encounter in Cape Cod. He told her that he planned to take a few days in Italy with Jane and then maybe go to America, 'but under guard'. He assured her that he was 'getting out of it'. It helped enormously that a new book was germinating, a book that he would eventually rate as one of his best.* 'Thank God the new book in my head begins to lift me.'

Another month passed before he wrote once more, with the news that he was 'up and running with the new book':

> I gave up all medication and advice, all shitty, and went to Panama alone which is where I want to set my new novel and after a few very sweaty nights I came alive and it's all right and it won't happen again, <u>it's all right</u>, & my heart and cock reach

---

* Published in 1996 as *The Tailor of Panama*.

for you, please don't fret anymore, I just had whatever it is you have once in your life and then never again ...

He asked her to forgive 'the awful silence'; and assured her that 'I'm not that person anymore and won't be again'. He pleaded with her not to be sad. 'I can't bear your sadness, inflicted by me.'

I went to Panama and it was everything you would have wanted it to be: demanding, absorbing, humid, risky, greedy, rackety (in both senses), rainy & absolutely the right place to be challenged & the right place for my story, which is everything I want: full of interior scope, and funny, and exciting. I took your advice & tried to think of myself first & last & get on with work, & not luxuriate in self examination, self flagellation ... And being alone was what I needed, even if at first it was very scary ...

Rather tactlessly, perhaps, he mentioned that several married women in Panama had made approaches to him (he would mention it again in a subsequent letter); though he assured her that he had resisted them – not least from fear of what their husbands might do to him if they found out. When he came back to England, he told her, 'the ghosts were waiting for me a bit – too much past that won't go away, so many sins,* all that.' Perhaps he was hinting that their affair had run its course. He apologised for the long silence,

but in a way it was the silence of age as well as isolation – at

---

* His handwriting here is especially difficult to decipher; this word may be 'sirens'.

63 there are days & nights & weeks when I desire nothing and no-one but some sort of reconciliation with my past, and that is denied me, very properly. And the useless truth is that bad acts can't be undone by remorse, & you have to find a way to forgive yourself, or you will die regretting everything.

In a letter dated 24 June 1995 he reported that he was 'writing like a beaver, shaping the story round what I saw, waiting to go again & see you on the way there or back'. He told her that 'I can't sleep for thinking about my book'.

A month later he wrote again. 'I'm mainly very calm, not taking anything, but I don't sleep much and the dreams are so death laden & awful – but I think that's always been the way with the writing; the moment a book starts to swell & preen itself, timor mortis* sets in.' He informed her that he would be coming to San Francisco to give a talk on 14 September. 'I'm flying straight in & out, with Jane, & my kids are coming up from Ojai,† so it isn't much of an opportunity to meet.' He still planned to go back to Panama, 'depending on when it's the right moment for the book, which is going so well I'm almost scared'. But there was no more talk of meeting on the way out or the way back. 'I feel close to you often Susan, I love you as a friend,' he wrote. 'If the fire's a bit low sometimes, that's bloody age and a lot of family stuff I won't bore you with.'

Susan felt that she had been given the brush-off; more than that, she felt that he had not been true to his feelings: that he had walked away from the kind of love that happens only once

---

* 'fear of death'.

† A small town and former hippie hangout in southern California, where David's son Stephen lives with his English wife Clarissa.

or twice in a lifetime. She was angry for a long time afterwards. After brooding on what had happened between them for over a year, she wrote to him again. This time the tradecraft failed. John Miller was no longer living at Sancreed, having distanced himself from David after his partner Michael had become jealous of their closeness. Her letter found its way to Tregiffian, where it was opened, and then forwarded to David at the chalet in Wengen, 'having caused its share of embarrassment'.

His reply was cold, with no endearment at the opening or the close. He found her portrait of what had happened between them 'unjust', and of his own character 'selective', and attempted a defence. 'I was greatly and truthfully moved by you, & remain so,' he wrote. 'We did indeed have much to share, much in common that was profound, fascinating & exciting'; but 'as the weeks went by I became increasingly certain that the interiority was for me unsustainable, and that to continue was to risk more than I was prepared to give up: the tranquillity in which to write, the privacy of my inner life, & the love of those around me'.

> I have the strongest memories of our meeting & they will
> be with me always; I love all the crazy and funny things that
> happen to you, and your courage and goodness, again; & your
> humour. But I have promised myself certain things too: a few
> more novels before I'm done, the continuity of the painful
> constricted life around me, and the resolution, somehow, of all
> the wrong turnings I have taken ...

Understandably she protested. To avoid further embarrassment she wrote c/o Rex Cowan, as instructed; but as Cowan happened to be in hospital, her letter was opened by his wife, who telephoned Jane and read her the contents: 'Hell followed.' This was life imitating art: in *The Tailor of Panama*, which had been published earlier that year, the eponymous tailor's wife throws a fit after discovering her husband's letters from his lover, Marta. When Susan came to read the novel, she recognised traces of herself in Marta; and found words that she had spoken to David replayed in Marta's speech.

In response to her protest, David wrote her one last letter:

> I wish you would not treat me as a lost faith Patient who only has to be comforted to be persuaded of his feelings. It isn't like that. I know what my feelings were – I was desperately in love with you. I know what they are – I'm 65, under the constant threat of running out of time and juice, I want to write a last (?) good novel, I want it to be my best. I live in a high-security household which suits my writing and my pathetic need to be left alone in guarded safety, I have not the time nor space for anything erratic, threatening, demanding that fucks up the creative clockwork (which simply seizes up when crises hit). I can't handle <u>the stuff</u>. For God's sake don't talk about coming over here & staying close – in the first place, I have no structure for independent movement, in the second I'm a lousy actor already under the heaviest suspicion, & in the third, you'd seize me up, for writing or anything else, such as feeling.

He offered another address to write to, and the prospect of meeting in California later in the year. But she refused to respond. It was over.

SIX

A bit stiff

In the early 1990s, the prospect of an unauthorised biography by the journalist Graham Lord brought David into contact with his former lover Liz Tollinton for the first time in many years. He telephoned her, sounding apprehensive and formal, obviously anxious to know whether she meant to co-operate with Lord. As it turned out she had initially agreed to do so, and then thought better of it. David served a writ on Lord, who was cowed into silence. Subsequently Liz and David lunched together. She was still young-looking, with unlined skin and a long, graceful neck, though now her hair was cut short and flecked with grey. Their affair had ended almost thirty years earlier, yet she had not stopped loving him. She had never married; she still wore his ring on her engagement finger. (Earlier she had met his first wife Ann for lunch in Selfridges to discuss how to respond to Lord's overtures, and had observed the pained look on Ann's face when she noticed the ring.) After the threat of the biography was lifted, Liz suffered a nervous breakdown.

'Do you mind as much as I do, all the publicity whenever he publishes a new book?' Liz had written to Susie Kennaway in 1983, around the time of publication of *The Little Drummer*

Girl. Later that year the two women had met for lunch, to discuss their reactions to a biography of James Kennaway that had just been published. She wrote to Susie afterwards:

> I felt rather sad somehow that even now we are not free of David – perhaps you are much more than I am, but I thought it true what you said to the effect that one will never know if one knew him, or if the person one thought one knew existed. Perhaps he goes around being other people's missing halves, and encourages them to project onto him what would make them complete, and then slips away, leaving one less complete than ever.

In 1992, after accosting him in the street, Liz had formed a friendship with Charles Pick, formerly managing director of William Heinemann, whom she had known in the 1960s, when she had been working for David as his secretary and Pick had been David's publisher. He had felt embittered when David had left for another publisher in 1970; his suggestion in the late 1980s of meeting for a drink had been rebuffed. There seems to have been only one subject of conversation during the several dinners Liz had with Pick. 'How David would have hated to know we had met,' she wrote to him after their first such evening; 'he once said that he did not like his friends meeting "behind his back" and one sees why.' She confessed to Pick that she had often contemplated suicide. After he had shown her several of the most upsetting letters he had received from David, she told him that she understood why David would not want them published, as 'they are far too revealing of himself'.

He seems to see-saw between the urge to reveal himself and to hide. I suppose he has affected our lives forever, and my parents could never forgive him, but even looking back now I would not want to be without the experience.

It was Pick who had given her name to Graham Lord.

In 1995, two years after the furore over the biography, Liz died of a heart attack, aged only fifty-eight. Her mother sent David an angry letter, accusing him of treating her 'wickedly and heartlessly'. He had stolen her daughter's youth, she wrote. 'It is to my infinite regret that she wore your ring until she died.'

*

Early in 1999, David's face appeared to Sue Dawson in a dream. 'I think we should see ourselves again,' he appeared to tell her. She had heard nothing from him for almost five years, since he had written to congratulate her on the publication of her novel, *The Forsytes*, a sequel to John Galsworthy's *The Forsyte Saga*. She had failed in various attempts to write a fictionalised version of her affair with David.

It so happened that David was due to give a talk at a theatre in London as part of a new literary festival, The Word. She decided to call at the box office on the off-chance that there might be a spare ticket, and there was; and so she found herself seated in the second row of the auditorium when David walked onto the stage. On his way to the lectern he paused and bowed in acknowledgement of the applause. After a few more steps he paused again and scanned the audience; and then gave a barely perceptible start as he spotted her.

After the talk she joined the long queue of those who had bought a copy of his latest novel, *Single & Single*, and were waiting for the author to inscribe it. When she reached him, he stood up to embrace her, and whispered 'Hello you' in her ear. As she offered him the book to sign, she slipped him a note of her new address and telephone number, which he surreptitiously pocketed.

He telephoned a few days later. 'My darling girl,' he said, 'are we still us?' He was about to go abroad, he told her; but on his return a few weeks later he came round to her North Kensington flat one lunchtime, laden with bags bearing flowers and delicious things to eat and drink: Stolichnaya vodka, Krug champagne, three types of cheese, biscuits, a baguette, a tin of foie gras and another of caviar, and a pork pie. They filled their champagne flutes and carried them through to the bedroom. 'We need new terms,' he suggested afterwards. 'I think we should just make it easy on ourselves. No more big promises.'

It had been fourteen years since they had last been together. By this time she was over forty; he was sixty-seven. His hair, which previously had been only speckled with grey, was now almost white. His face was essentially unchanged, but there were lines of strain around the eyes. She noticed that his top lip was pulled back, so that he appeared to be smiling. 'But it wasn't a smile of contentment,' she would write later: 'more a rictus of resignation.' His stomach, which had been flat, had developed a paunch.

As they ate the picnic he had brought he described the new novel he was writing, an attack on the practices of 'Big Pharma'. This was the book that would be published in 2001 under the title *The Constant Gardener*. He told her that he had sold the flat in St John's Wood to his friend William Shawcross. They talked about their loves, and he mentioned only one significant affair in the intervening years, with an American photographer who had approached him at a publicity event in Washington. The way he told it, she had cleverly established that he was there on his own by asking if 'Mrs Cornwell' was available for a photograph. 'It was quite a good stunt,' he told Sue: 'I liked that.' Though he does not seem to have told her this, he had taken the American photographer with him to meet his sister Charlotte on a visit to England, and on another occasion to meet John Margetson, one of his oldest friends. They used to talk a lot on the telephone. One day Jane had come to David querying a telephone bill. 'We don't know anyone with this number, do we?' she had asked.

There had been an awkward pause. 'I don't think that I am accountable to you for the phone calls I make,' he had replied. He explained to Sue what had ensued. 'Well, the atmosphere was frosty for a few days.'

He mentioned 'some other minor encounters, only a few and all *en passant*', which seems an odd way to describe his epistolary love affair with Susan Anderson, which had lasted almost two years. But this was only one of several misleading statements David seems to have made to Sue about other women. He allowed her to believe that, apart from with her, all his other love affairs since Susie Kennaway had been conducted abroad, which was simply untrue. He added to the inscription in the book she had bought when she came to his talk: 'John le Carré – was born again soon after this predestined encounter, following fourteen years solitary, loyally served.' Of course, this reference to 'fourteen years solitary' was nonsense: he had conducted at least three serious affairs during those fourteen years, and probably others that have not been revealed.

One love affair, undoubtedly more than *en passant*, was with an Italian woman: a writer, critic and actress, then in her early forties. She was recently widowed, after her husband had been killed in an accident. David met her in Capri, where he had gone to pick up an award at a ceremony that she presided over. Afterwards he wrote to her, and they began an affair. She already had a lover, but she discarded him to be with David. She would inspire the character of Katya in *The Russia House* (1989), the courageous and principled young woman for whom the English protagonist Barley Blair risks everything.

As I mentioned in the introduction, I had been in touch with both the Italian journalist and the American photographer, and discovered quite a lot about their relationships with David, but neither wished to be identified publicly and I have chosen to respect their wishes.

Another affair, short-lived but intense, began in the early 1990s, after a fan had called at Tregiffian and left her address while the Cornwells were away. I learned about her from Nicholas Shakespeare, who had heard about her from David himself. She was an American woman, who lived in Baton Rouge, just up the Mississippi river from New Orleans. David was looking for another affair, so he wrote to her, and she wrote back; then he concocted a reason for a research trip to Louisiana. She met him at the airport, and they made an instant connection. 'It's like we've known each other all our lives,' he told a friend afterwards: 'she was my ideal reader.' It turned out that she was married to her childhood sweetheart, a lawyer, a paraplegic since a car crash only three weeks after their wedding. After four nights together in a New Orleans hotel, she took him home for the weekend. David found the situation unbearably awkward, and when she crept into his bedroom at night and stripped off her clothes, he told her, 'I can't.' They took a drive together, and David said, 'If we go on driving, I can be with you forever.' This was her turn to say that she couldn't. At the end of the trip, when she saw him off, they promised to meet in Europe. The plan was for her to abscond from a package tour to Marseilles to meet him, but when it came to the point, he couldn't face it. He sent her a parting gift of a Victorian necklace. 'Maybe we were both looking for our own way out,' he told Nicholas Shakespeare afterwards. 'But you need a bourgeois woman like Jane. She's the only woman I can write around.'

It was true that there were *some* 'minor encounters'. One of these was with a local young woman who spent a night at Tregiffian. Trying to find the light, she instead pressed an alarm switch linked to the police station. David had been woken by the sound of banging on the door. He stumbled downstairs and found policemen and a local farmer, all concerned for his safety. The young woman had slept through it all.

His affair with Sue resumed much as it had been before, only now they met at her flat rather than his. David read her pages from his new book in bed, as he had done while he was writing *A Perfect Spy*. He now had a different dead letter box in Cornwall, c/o a new friend, Dave Humphries, a television writer. He also had a mobile phone, which made it much easier to call Sue than it had been the last time around. Quite quickly they settled into a routine, as before, only slightly different. 'We're married, you and I,' he told her as he left the flat late one afternoon after they had spent the day together. But there was no more talk about leaving his wife. He spoke as if they had missed their opportunity. 'We should have moved in together, you and I,' he said, 'and fuck the lot of them.'

'You were my best shot at it,' he continued, 'getting out of the slammer. But I can't leave a sixty-two-year-old woman now.'

David's daily life had become more circumscribed. Rainer Heumann had died in 1996, and Authors Workshop, the Swiss-based company that David had used as a device to minimise tax, had been wound up the following year. He was less independent now that his expenditure was more closely scrutinised. For another trip to Switzerland Sue was obliged to make the arrangements herself, using a wad of cash he had given her. Once again she flew alone to Geneva, where David met her at the airport, and they took a train to Lausanne together. In their hotel room they made love with porn playing on the television screen.

They caught a ferry across to the French side of the lake and had lunch in a restaurant, sitting outside. Afterwards they strolled in the countryside. In a meadow spotted with flowers Sue sat down with her back to a tree, while David sat in the sun, his arms around his knees. They talked about his new book, and how his hero was on a journey to find out who had killed his wife. 'Another chap on his personal odyssey,' she suggested. Sue was startled when David asked her why Odysseus had set out on his odyssey in the first place: not least because he had asked her the very same question fifteen years before, on a beach in Lesbos. It occurred to her that David was like Odysseus, always trying to find his way home.*

Jane was suspicious when David returned from Switzerland,

---

* David told me that Jane had given him an embroidered picture of Penelope standing on the shore, 'waving her man into the distance & wishing him Godspeed'. He asked for a sentence I had written describing this in my biography to be deleted.

as he informed Sue during a telephone call. 'So we'll just have to be careful,' he warned. They next met when he arrived at her flat after seeing his wife off on a train to Cornwall. After two glasses of ice-cold vodka, David began to speculate on what it would be like if they were together all the time. 'The floodgates would open,' he said. 'I'd write all the time.' She was startled when he asked if she wanted children. 'I think you'd make a marvellous mother,' he went on, 'especially if you had a boy.' She asked what he would do if she became pregnant. 'Leave,' he replied unhesitatingly. 'Join you to look after the nipper.'

David spent the month of August in Tregiffian with his family. He would telephone her while out on his daily walk, often having to search for a signal. He and Sue were due to leave on 1 September for Berne, his refuge when he had run away from his boarding school at the age of sixteen, and then on to Elba. As before, he had given her a wad of cash to buy the tickets. This way of doing things had begun to rankle with her. One day he called after she had spent a stressful morning trying and failing to make the necessary bookings. When he enquired whether she had bought her ticket yet, she asked him irritably if he couldn't find a way to have just one credit card that his wife didn't know about.

There was a long pause at the other end of the line. 'I think that's a bit stiff—' he said at last, and quickly rang off. She never spoke to him again. She tried to telephone him several times, but he did not pick up. She wrote to him, to the two dead letter boxes he had given her, in London and in Cornwall; and eventually received a reply, in which he made it clear that he had decided to settle for the life he had, which was 'not the worst'.

*

In June 2001, in the months before his seventieth birthday, David wrote a letter to his sons about what he wanted to happen when he died. 'I had an amazing life, against the odds,' he wrote. 'I turned from a bad man to a much better one.'

> Jane's loyalty and love, and her love for all of you, have been my mainstay. That she prevailed against my infidelities & bad moods, that she preserved her own integrity, that she made our marriage work through thick & thin, became the source of our happiness. Nobody could have been a better partner and friend, nobody could have helped me better to fulfil whatever talent I possessed, than Jane.

In February 2003 David wrote Jane a love letter. 'My love, my darling love,' he addressed her:

> You gave me my life. You taught me the only kind of love that matters. I have grown so close to you in my heart in these recent years that I cannot believe we shall ever be divided. No number of 'sorry's can wipe away my disloyalties; no amount of 'thank you's can express my thanks. But the love you have taught me is indestructible, and in the face of it, everything else is diminished. We did a good job with our lives by the end. We were decent people. My darling, I love you, & I always, always shall.

We don't know how Jane responded to this moving tribute. If she was not as touched as she might have been otherwise, that could well have been because he had written to her in similar terms before, in 1987, and had conducted at least three serious love affairs since.

In 2006, in a nightclub in eastern Congo, where he had gone to research his novel *The Mission Song*, David became involved in a spat with the writer and journalist Michela Wrong, who was showing him around this dangerous part of the world. 'You've used the term "womaniser" twice now, as a pejorative,' he complained. It struck Michela as a strange thing to notice and retain, particularly as she hadn't been talking about him when she used the term. She felt that she had touched a nerve: if David smarted to hear the term used in this way, perhaps this was because he feared it might be used of him. The next morning they apologised to each other, and made up, but what he had said remained with her: a hint that he might not have been the most faithful of husbands.

*

In 2006 David received a letter from Verity Ravensdale, concerned about a possible biography of her husband Nicholas Mosley, and what it might reveal. She wanted to confer with him about 'the best way of conducting things'. David's reply was sent from Edinburgh, where he had gone to be with his son Tim, then recovering from a severe manic depressive episode. 'I have no idea of course what biographies/autobiographies are being contemplated here,' David replied,

> but I'll never read them, & I certainly won't contribute to them, by word or deed, anywhere. That's the only way I know. Nobody will get a word out of me – or Jane – now or ever.
>
> I look back on the times we shared & remember the good bits with joy. I don't think we did anyone much harm, as it happened, except perhaps ourselves. The hardest bit – perhaps

the impossible bit – is to remember who one was at the time. And that's where all the after-the-fact junk starts to get nasty.

His reply to a subsequent letter from Verity was noticeably tetchy. 'It's very hard for me to receive personal letters without attracting interest, so please don't write again,' he told her.

> I've no idea from your letters who is writing what. In principle, I hate the idea, whether it's about myself, or anybody I know … The collateral damage is <u>always</u> uncontrollable, & wretchedly unfair: good marriages that have held together in spite of everything are made to look tawdry, children are wounded and alienated, and a few old people get their rocks off, and the press picks at the carcass of it all …

He offered to telephone her in a few days' time. In a further letter, he told her that he had tried unsuccessfully to call her two or three times. 'Who is writing what when? Could you please write me a letter to London … in an unobtrusive envelope, typed, not marked personal, telling me what is planned, & suggesting when I can call you …'

He apologised for 'all this hole-in-corner nonsense, but … I am most concerned to protect Jane's feelings.' In the event, nothing ensued: the biography of Mosley contained no mention of his wife's affair with David.

*

There would be at least one more love affair, with a woman less than half his age, though this one seems to have been platonic. Two years after their affair ended, she tried to make contact with him again, but he rebuffed her, just as he rebuffed the Italian journalist when she approached him a decade or so after the end of their affair.

By now in his seventies, he may have lost some of his enthusiasm for the chase. He continued writing up until the end, but it is perhaps not a coincidence that the novels became less interesting and more formulaic. Without a new muse for each book, his inspiration dried up.

SEVEN

An inspector calls

I described in the introduction to this book how I came to write David's biography, and the basis on which we agreed it should be done, 'at arm's length'. I stressed to him at the outset that 'I must be seen to be independent; I must be free to make my own judgements; I must be in control of my own book'; though I did accept his stipulation that he should have the opportunity to read the text before I submitted it to the publishers, both to correct factual errors and to advise whether 'any passages should be amended or removed on the basis that they do not give due respect to the sensitivities of living third parties'. I did not then appreciate that the living party whose sensitivities most required respect would turn out to be David himself.

After protracted negotiation, conducted, appropriately enough, at arm's length via our respective agents, we reached a formal agreement in November 2010. By the time the contract was signed I had already flown over to Seattle to see David's brother Tony, knowing that he was ill with cancer and might not live much longer. I had also met his half-sister Charlotte, and together we had been to visit her mother Jean (David's step-mother) in her care home.

'One Adam Sisman, who has written an excellent and much lauded biography of Hugh Trevor-Roper, is going to write mine, and reckons it will take him four years,' David wrote to his old friend John Margetson, whom he had known since they had met on the same MI6 training course more than half a century earlier. 'I'm staying as far away from it as I can,' he continued: 'but I like him, and welcome his endeavour, however painful & embarrassing in the short term.'

'I have put my trust in him,' David wrote to Susie Kennaway, who had written to check whether she would have his consent to talk to me. 'I have <u>no</u> editorial control over what he writes, beyond checking dates, places & bald facts.' In an email to Martin Pick, son of his publisher Charles Pick, David stressed that the biography 'is emphatically not an authorised one'. Instead, he wrote, 'it is a warts-and-all biography,* which seems to me the only sort worth bothering with.'

Over the next few years I had half a dozen or so day-long sessions with David, in which I was able to interrogate him in detail about his past. These amounted to perhaps fifty hours in total. The normal pattern was for me to arrive at his house in Hampstead at around eleven in the morning, to talk for a couple of hours, and then head off for lunch, usually in his local pub. Afterwards we would go back to his house, and continue until early evening, with a fortifying drink in the late afternoon. I enjoyed his company, which was always stimulating and often fun, though I was a little disappointed by what he had to say. Much of what he told me consisted of generalities, and often stories with which I was already familiar – some of

---

* Later he would complain that it was 'all warts and no all'.

which I suspected to be exaggerated, or maybe even fabricated.

Only now does it occur to me that David may have failed to understand the function of these sessions. For me, they were a guide to further investigations, as well as a source of anecdotal detail. For him, as later became apparent, they were a form of dictation. When eventually he was able to read what I had written, he seemed surprised that I had not transcribed much of what he told me verbatim. He was accustomed to interviews with journalists, in which what he said would be recorded and printed. He would also express surprise that I had not taped our sessions, perhaps forgetting that he had stipulated at the start that I should not do so.

At a late stage in the process he asked for a 'right to a reply' to anything in the biography which he found objectionable. I resisted this request. For the subject to want to contribute to the content seemed to me to show a misunderstanding of the nature of biography – or at least, of the kind of biography that I wanted to write.

As well as visiting David in London, I made several visits to Tregiffian, where I would work in his archive, and take my meals with David and Jane when they were there too. Though his records were chaotic and far from complete, I found there the factual foundation on which to build my biography. There was even a long document that he had written in 1968 for a psychiatrist about his sexual history, which I suspect that David might have forgotten. I also worked in other archives, particularly the Bodleian Library in Oxford, which held the typescripts of David's books – except *The Little Drummer Girl*, which had found its way to Austin, Texas. From these it was possible to trace the development of each novel from the earliest draft of the opening chapter to the final proof of the whole. I was intrigued to discover that the earliest drafts were often significantly different from the finished books. The first draft of *Tinker Tailor Soldier Spy*, for example, begins with a character called Billy, an early version of Jim Prideaux. Rather than working as a temporary schoolmaster in a West Country preparatory school, Billy is living on a Cornish cliff, embittered and alone. As the book opens he is holding a bucket in his hand, on his way to feed the chickens; he has paused to stare up at a black car weaving down the hillside towards him. This brings 'Rod' Tarr, the troubled Chief of the Intelligence Service, known as 'the Tank', who suspects the existence of a mole within the Service. In this early draft Billy is interrogated by Tarr in a safe house, just as in the finished version Tarr (now a completely different character with the first name Ricki) is questioned by Smiley.

Many valuable records had been lost. Rainer Heumann's archives had been sent to landfill after the death of his widow, for example. I was dismayed to discover that David himself had destroyed his correspondence with Jack Geoghegan, his first American publisher, the man who had done more than anybody else to advance David's career. He and David had been close, and Geoghegan's son told me that his father had kept a photograph of David on his desk until the day he died.

I was given introductions to current and former friends (some now enemies), former colleagues, and members of David's family. One contact led to another: on the Essex shoreline I clambered along the shingle, and in Southern California I strolled along a track into the scrub. In a single month I flew to Germany four times, on each occasion returning the same day.

JOHN LE CARRÉ

9 Gainsborough gdns
NW3 1BJ

21 Jan 2012

Dear Adam,

Thanks for yours, which
I greatly appreciated, + the more so
since I was laid low by some
lurgy yet to be defined, + sitting
in Cornwall feeling sorry for self,
+ staring at an infuriatingly
uncooperative manuscript, version
500, + still nowhere near.

You asked me: how do I know
when it's right, when do the
bells ring? And actually, "it's

The first two pages of a letter from David Cornwell to me,
21 January 2012. He was responding to a question I had asked after
reading successive drafts of his novels in the Bodleian Library.

2

a question we ask of all creative people – musicians, painters, sculptors etc. – when do you know it's hit the mark? – & the only answer any of them can give is, 'because I do.' But I'm glad you found some response in the Gregoriev interrogation, which really is a matter of cadence & timing, & the tightrope between comedy & serious intent.

While I was feeling sorry for yself I kept abreast of the critical acclaim your 'Hugh' was receiving in the US, & was very pleased by it. And of course, I was tickled

I began to feel like George Smiley, patiently reconstructing the past from surviving fragments. I became aware that some of my interviewees were reporting back to David on what had been said. From time to time I would receive a chatty letter from him, often with greetings of some kind, with news of what had been happening in his world.

In January 2012 David wrote to me after a period of being 'laid low by some lurgy yet to be defined'. As usual, both the letter itself and the envelope were handwritten, suggesting that nobody else knew what he had written, perhaps not even that he had written to me at all. He had passed much of the time thinking about the biography, he told me, and asking himself what he felt about it. Here, as at other times in our correspondence, I had the sense that he was thinking aloud as much as he was trying to communicate anything to me.

> Wherever you've been, you've left a benign impression, for which already I am very grateful. I can't imagine how I will come out of it, but I think that's what drew me into it: the notion that this was never something I could do for myself, & that somehow, whatever the outcome, this was going to be a gift of sorts to my children; a gift of truth, insofar as there ever is one, & it can be told.

David used the same expression, of my book as a gift to his children, in a letter to his brother Tony, written around the same time. It was odd, he wrote, 'to have an "Inspector Calls" in one's life, going round ringing doorbells from one's past, & not always coming up with very edifying results: my love-life has always been a disaster area, & without Jane I wd long ago have gone down with the ship.' He added that 'with luck, the

Grim Reaper will have edited me out, before he (Adam) ever gets around to publishing'.

If David found the experience odd, I did too. It was slightly disconcerting to spend so much time with a writer whose work was already so familiar to me, over such a long time. I wondered if I might read the books in a different way after such prolonged exposure to the man who had written them. In my mind I began to distinguish between David Cornwell and John le Carré.

Towards the end of that year, Nicholas Shakespeare told me about the Italian journalist with whom David had had an affair. As I have already mentioned in the introduction, I sent her a tactful letter, and received a polite response, indicating that my informant had been mistaken. I had also identified (after one false start) the woman with whom David had fallen in love while serving in Bonn, the wife of one of his colleagues. I was especially keen to see any letters he might have written to her, because their affair had taken place while he was writing *The Spy Who Came in from the Cold*, the book that would change his life forever. It occurred to me that the two might be connected; and even if they were not, his love letters might provide some insight into his state of mind at this turning-point in his career. I appreciated that she was by this time an old lady, still married to the same husband, and I therefore wrote to her in coded terms; but even this discreet approach was enough to send her into a panic, and to contact David. The ensuing fuss brought about the first crisis in our relations. He sent me a letter marked 'Private and Personal', of which, he told me, he had not kept a copy. 'I have never disguised from you –' he wrote, 'or from my family, in principle – that my love life has been at best "untidy", & at worst – though I don't expect I said this – near suicidal.'

I doubt whether I need to tell you how difficult this letter is for me to write. I admire your work & your tenacity; I would wish that in your position I would show the same acumen; I have a genuine respect for your tact & integrity. But I also have a sense, on the strength of recent experience, of impending disaster in my life – i.e. in the lives of those I hold most dear – and I can't allow any more time to pass without expressing it to you, and indicating to you the heavy footmarks of your recent explorations.

David proposed that we should revise the terms of our agreement, so that the biography should be 'authorised'. Of course I was familiar with the term, but I was never entirely sure what he meant by it, beyond his having more say over what I wrote, and so I resisted any change. As I had done from the start, I argued that the biography would be less credible if it were seen to have been under his control.

We met soon afterwards to discuss how to proceed. 'As you may imagine, I have thought ceaselessly about our conversation – & about little else,' he wrote to me afterwards. (Again he told me that he had kept no copy of this letter.) 'I never doubted that this part of my life would loom large, or that in some form I wanted it to be aired: a gift of truth to my children, as I wrote to you, and that means no shying away ... The question therefore is <u>how</u>.'

David proposed that the subject of his infidelities should be dealt with in general terms, without naming names, which seemed to me a reasonable solution in the circumstances. There was an appendix to this letter: a note that listed the reasons for his philandering.* It ended with a disquieting postscript:

---

* The text of the note is reproduced on pages 41–2.

It is no coincidence that in 'Spy', 'A Perfect Spy' and 'A Constant Gardener' [*sic*] the protagonist kills himself. Ditto 'The Tailor of Panama'. Enough?

Of course I was alarmed. Not only was my project at risk; my subject was hinting that he might kill himself.

So I was relieved to receive a much calmer letter from David only three days later, in which he mentioned that he and Jane were on the brink of leaving for a holiday in Provence. 'I need a bit of space & time,' he wrote, but he hoped to meet soon after his return. 'I confess to being a bit thrown by all these accusing ghosts from my past,' he continued, '& I hope will be in better shape to talk to you when we return.' A fortnight later I received a further friendly letter, suggesting a meeting in the following month.

I began to recognise a pattern, in which David would become agitated – sometimes very agitated – but quickly calm down and recover his composure.

I continued to work on the book, and to have occasional meetings with David. I had decided at the start that I should not hide anything from him, so I told him during one of our meetings that I had spoken to Sue Dawson. 'Oh, God!' he groaned.

Sometime in 2013 David announced that he was contemplating a memoir. I remember trying to think through the ramifications of this while walking across Hampstead Heath on a lovely summer evening, after spending the day with him. I was concerned, particularly by the possibility that his memoir might appear before my biography, and perhaps overshadow it. Naturally he acknowledged the force of this argument, but urged me to 'hurry up, because I won't live forever'. After some consideration I outlined a scheme which would allow me to publish a cut-down version of my biography in the autumn of 2014, a year earlier than planned. It would concentrate on the first sixty years of his life, with only an epilogue covering the years since the end of the Cold War. I would publish a second, revised edition after his death, dealing with the last period of his life in full. My publishers were not keen on this plan, but they were willing to go along with it if it meant being able to publish the biography before the memoir.

In December 2013 I received an email from Jane:

> We know you hope to publish in autumn 2014 and that we shall hear from you at Christmas whether that is definitely so. We both appreciate your very diligent approach to his work and life – and I'm sure you must have sensed that we hold you in warm regard and esteem, as do all the family members you have talked to. You have won not only our respect but also the interest and support of everybody. My anxiety is that the constant pressure for more sessions with David, may make him feel that he has to draw a line and say, that's enough.

By early 2014 the first volume was almost complete. David arranged for me to meet Jane without him at their house in Hampstead, in order to discuss various subjects, including a passage I had written about how she and David had met, and another about David's working methods. On the unwritten agenda was the topic of his infidelities: a topic which I found embarrassing, and she surely must have found humiliating.

It was 9.30 in the morning when I arrived, an hour and a half earlier than I usually met David. He greeted me at the door and ushered me into the little living room where we had often conducted our interviews. Then Jane appeared, and David left the room, and a moment or two later I heard the slam of the front door. This was the first time that Jane and I had been alone together for more than a few moments. I felt awkward, and she seemed tense; neither of us wanted to be having this talk. We began by discussing the drafts I had sent her. Then, rather abruptly, the conversation moved on to the topic which I had been dreading and neither of us really wanted to discuss. She uttered some lines which had evidently been rehearsed, which I dutifully copied into my notebook. 'Nobody can have all of David,' she told me. I had little doubt that everything she said had been dictated by David beforehand. There was no real discussion. The session seemed artificial, and I think that both of us were relieved to draw it to a close. I mumbled my goodbyes and left, without seeing David again. I imagined that he was lurking on the Heath, and would not return to the house until sure that I was gone.

I recognised a similar situation when I came to read a passage in Sue Dawson's memoir, where she describes how David arranged for her to meet his former lover Yvette Pierpaoli over lunch. He introduced the two women at a French restaurant in St John's Wood, and then left them alone together. Sue seems to have found this almost as uncomfortable as I had found my morning with Jane. 'It felt to me then as though we were two characters in search of an author,' she wrote – rather wittily, as it seemed to me.

It was evident that the question of how I would write about his personal life was very much in David's mind. A few weeks after I had seen Jane I received another letter from him. 'I trust you, & I think you trust me,' he assured me; but he sought 'to clarify what you will be writing, or not writing, about my extra-marital affairs during my two marriages, and to reach agreement on how best to handle the subject'.

> Jane & I find the mounting uncertainty & stress close-on unbearable ... an increasingly dark cloud threatens my work and – as it seems to us at this juncture – our domestic peace ... we feel we are living with a ticking bomb.

Once more he suggested 'changing the terms of engagement', to make mine an authorised biography. He referred to the second volume, to be published ten years on, which I took to mean after his death. 'I would be very happy to help in the making of it, if it enables you to leave until later the worst & maddest things. In other words, you hold over the issue of my love life for a decade.'

A few weeks later I sent him the text of my biography, complete except for the epilogue and the introduction.* This was the start of a long struggle. Though I never expected it to be easy, I had not anticipated how difficult it would turn out to be. In particular, I had not imagined that he would want to engage so closely with my text, given what he had said at the outset. At times I felt as if I might lose control of my own book.

His response showed that he was having second thoughts about my scheme. Though he did not say as much, he may have felt that a biography that concentrated on the first sixty years of his life would lend strength to the argument that he had lost his subject when the Cold War ended, a criticism to which he was

---

* This version consisted of twenty chapters; the published book, of twenty-five.

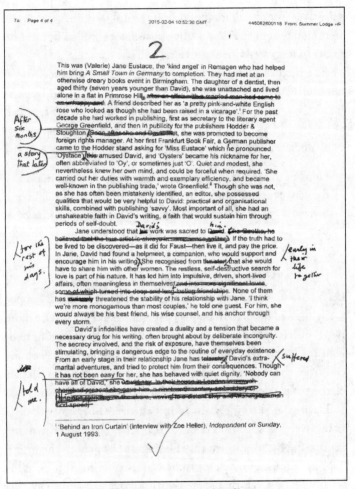

Typescript page of my biography of le Carré,
with David Cornwell's corrections.

sensitive. 'Your book might profit by telling people at the outset that I am part of the time we live in and not simply a figure who exists in forgotten literary reviews and old scandals.'

In a further letter, written a fortnight later, he expressed disappointment with the book in its existing form. 'Your book as it stands is not doing its job,' he wrote. 'In consequence I, as well as you, could be the sufferer. You can't expect me to enjoy, least of all applaud, my own trivialisation.'

> None of this diminishes in the least my affection and respect for you, which are shared by all the family. It is simply ... I don't believe that you have yet achieved the symmetry and balance that, for instance, informed your excellent 'Hugh'.
>
> Forgive this outburst, but if not now, when?

I took the train down to Cornwall and spent a day with David discussing the issues he had raised. By now he had temporarily shelved his plan to publish a memoir, so there was no more need for haste. We agreed to revert to the original plan of publishing a full biography on the original schedule. In a telephone call from the train back from Penzance I explained this further change of plan to my understanding publishers.

David was showing signs of impatience to begin work on a new novel. His son Simon now took on the role of intermediary, cautioning me over lunch that David's anxiety about the imminent appearance of my biography was distracting him from his writing. Simon felt that some breathing space would enable his father to relax. Later in the year he would travel from London to visit me at my house in Bristol, and it was then that he first raised the notion of a 'secret annexe'.

I sent David the completed typescript of the biography at the end of the year 2014, my original deadline. He had asked that this and subsequent drafts were sent via a secure server, presumably fearing that someone might intercept them, which seemed to me unlikely. On 2 January 2015 I received his initial response, a letter marked 'Personal & Confidential'. He had not finished reading the typescript, but already appeared anxious. 'I cannot continue to help you with your book unless you assure me that the undertakings you gave me at the outset stand fast, & you will honour them,' he wrote.

> There are many passages in the book that I wish to dispute. There are glaring omissions that seem almost deliberate. There are a string of small calumnies and one or two large ones. There are inaccuracies.
>
> But above all there are passages – two or three at present count – that are simply too painful, too unbearable for me personally, and for my family, and its most fragile members.

As I mentioned in the introduction, David wanted me to eliminate all that I had written about Liz Tollinton; and the passage about Derek Johns, which he took to be a veiled hint at homosexual yearnings. He took particular umbrage at what seemed to me an innocuous passage in my introduction. I had described the biography as 'a work-in-progress', referring to the fact that David was still active in his eighty-fourth year, 'perhaps as active as he had ever been': more might be expected from him. I mentioned a plan to publish a revised and updated edition in due course; and asked anyone who felt that they might have anything to contribute to write to me, care of my publishers. For David, 'the most disingenuous addition to the book is the introduction, which takes the opportunity to solicit more material of the sort we shall

Personal & Confidential

London   1
2 Jan 2015

Dear Adam,

    I had best keep this short.
I cannot continue to help you with
your book until you assure me
that the undertakings you gave me
at the outset stand fast, & you
will honour them.

    There are many passages in
the book I wish to dispute. There are
glaring omissions that almost seem
deliberate. There are a string
of small calumnies and one or
two large ones. There are inaccuracies.

    But above all there are
passages — two or three at
present count — that are

Letter from David Cornwell to me, 2 January 2015.

<u>Personal & Confidential.</u> № 2

Simply too painful, too unbearable for me personally, and for my family, and its most fragile members.

As before, you write me as if I was dead. You permit me no right of reply, no other side to the frequently malicious observations of your witnesses, whose testimony you have not once tested against mine. Everything I say must be found wanting at best —(but then I didn't say it to <u>you</u>.) where you need to disparage me — a constant need — there is always that theoretical 'cynic' or 'sceptic' on hand to put in the knife.

Personal & Confidential.   3

Perhaps the most disingenuous

addition to the book is the

introduction, which takes the

opportunity to solicit more material

of the sort we shall quickly

infer; and at the same time

manages to imply that the

book has my blessing, &

is even some sort of joint

effort. Neither is true at present.

I look forward to receiving

your assurances.

As ever

David.

P.S. In your email, just arrived,
you ask whether you can show the book to
other readers meantime. I ask you <u>on no
account</u> to do this. Dad.

quickly infer; and at the same time manages to imply that the book has my blessing, & is even some sort of joint effort.' (I recognised no such inference or implication.) He asked me not to show the typescript to any other reader until we had talked further.

This letter was followed by a longer one ten days later: seventeen handwritten pages, plus four pages of appendices. But though the length was daunting, I was reassured by the content. Many of the points he raised were details easily resolved: for example, asking for derogatory references in old private letters to 'Krauts' and 'Huns' to be deleted, for the sake of his German readership; though 'I am, always shall be, like most people of my generation, wary of Germany ...'

> In the large, as your reader, & an admiring one, I think it's a 'fair, scrupulous and successful book' that will add lustre to your name, if not to mine; or not with the same certainty by any means ... Do I want it published in my lifetime, even in this form? No. But I <u>didn't</u> know that going in.

He detected in my narrative a sceptical tone, 'that causes us to question your objectivity'. As an example, he cited a passage I had written about his refusal of the offer of a knighthood, which I had contrasted with the willingness of other writers, some who expressed radical opinions, to accept establishment honours. He seemed to suspect that I was in some unstated manner disparaging his decision, though my intention had been the opposite; I meant to praise him, not to bury him. 'I have noted, I hope, in the ts. other moments where I think you are gratuitously skeptical of my motives,' he wrote, 'just as I have frequently applauded the many moments when I think you have hit the nail on the head.'

In my text I had remarked on his ruthlessness in his dealings with publishers and agents, several of whom had mistakenly come to regard him as a friend.

I think you miss the point that my perception of entrepreneurs was derived in large part from Ronnie's court, & I saw myself (not always wrongly by any means) as fighting a lone battle against an unscrupulous cartel of corporate publishers and embedded literary agents.

On the contrary, my research suggested that he had left a trail of hurt and wounded publishers and agents in his wake: Jack Geoghegan and Charles Pick, for example.

As for his personal life,

My affairs, I suspect, were a lot like anyone else's: each a journey into new territory, each an escape from the last, each offering a refuge from I don't know what – perhaps convention itself – and, in my case, each a vain attempt to find the Ur-woman I never had, never understood, and always suspected by definition.

At this late stage he urged that the book should be postponed – 'and the reasons could be entirely professional: namely, that 2015/2016 are sensational years in my career'. He mentioned that he was writing a play about his father, which he hoped would be staged by the Almeida Theatre early in 2016. (This was shelved after a lack of enthusiasm from the artistic director.)

I finished a novel,* but it had no heart to it, & once it was

---

* Presumably a reference to the posthumously published *Silverview* (2021).

completed, I put it aside without showing it to Jonny or any professional – certainly no publisher. I <u>don't</u> blame you, only myself, but in retrospect it's pretty clear to me that my (exaggerated) apprehensions about the biography played a part. Or so it seems now. Perhaps, though, I'm written out, so far as the novel is concerned.*

He ended on a plaintive note. 'I would give anything to have this book deferred, because I don't know how I'm going to live with it for the rest of my life.'

For my part, I had begun to feel divided in two, as Ian Hamilton described in his *In Search of J. D. Salinger*. There was 'me grappling feebly with the moral issues' and 'my biographizing alter ego, now my constant companion, merely eager to get on with the job'.

On 4 February 2015 David wrote to me with alterations to two especially sensitive passages about his infidelities. 'If you are able to accept the changes as they stand, and eliminate entirely the Tollinton passage, which is a separate issue,' he said, 'then I am in agreement with your suggestion that you show the book to your chosen readers immediately.' Not for the first time, he mentioned Jane's concern 'that she shd not appear to have been

---

* In fact he would publish two more novels and one memoir in his lifetime. In October 2021 *The Times*, reporting on a speech given at the weekend by David's agent Jonny Geller at the Cheltenham Literary Festival, suggested that David had been 'so disrupted' by my impending biography that 'it put him off course' ('How John le Carré's biographer put last novel on ice'). I responded in a letter, published the next day. At the memorial service for David and Jane a few days later, Geller sought me out and told me that he had been misquoted ('I agreed with everything in your letter').

complicit in my affairs, or to have condoned them; to the contrary, she suffered greatly, but endured'. He warned that these were not the last of his proposed changes:

> There will be many other points, I am sure, that will arise in the editing, and you have assured me that I shall have the opportunity to speak again when the book is at a later stage. In the meantime I suggest we scrub the proposed London meeting next week, and have a moratorium.

Discussions continued through subsequent drafts, even after the book was copy-edited. Belatedly I remembered that David was in the habit of rewriting his own books in proof, a privilege denied to most authors. On 1 May 2015 Jane sent me by email a typed, twenty-two-page memorandum from David, containing 196 numbered points. Most of them were straightforward enough, though it was unusual to be contemplating further changes at this late stage, and introduced the risk of error as a result. Sometimes the discussion was circular: on at least one occasion, for example, I was able to demonstrate to him that a source that he had questioned was himself.* He complained that I had written about an episode – his visit to the 'Villa Brigitte', where he had interviewed a young German woman accused of acts of terrorism against Israeli officials – that he had intended to

---

* 'You asked me in your list of the questions what my source was for saying that you had "fallen out of love" with Ronnie, and at the time I couldn't remember, so I took this out; but I have just stumbled across it, at the beginning of the last section of your wonderful *New Yorker* article, "In Ronnie's court". I'm not proposing that it should go back in, but I didn't want you to think that I might have invented it!' Letter from me to David, 19 May 2015.

reserve for his memoir. I pointed out that he had already drawn on this story in his fiction, as a chapter in *The Secret Pilgrim*. He seemed disgruntled, a tone that I found reflected in private letters that I did not see until they were published in volume form towards the end of 2022. In one of these, to Tom Stoppard, he described my book as 'an elephantine work of ballbreaking banality – but otherwise conscientious, fact-based, and, for me, a horrible mirror'. (There was an irony that he should write in such terms to Stoppard, because at an earlier stage in our relationship, David had offered himself as broker in negotiating for me to write Stoppard's biography – an offer of help that he was unable to deliver, as I well knew.)*

As for me, I felt worn down by the seemingly unending whittling away at what I had written, and by this time my overriding motive was simply to get to the end of the process, one way or another.

After such a bruising experience I was pleasantly surprised to receive a friendly letter from David on the day my biography was published in October 2015. 'I'm sure you're having a great time, so enjoy it,' he wrote, with only a slight edge: 'What's done is done.'

*

Ten days earlier, it had been announced that David had revived his plan to publish a memoir. 'He's trying to wrest back control of the agenda,' commented my editor. Since then it has often been

---

* As it turned out, Stoppard's biography would be written by Hermione Lee. In contrast to David, Stoppard refrained from trying to control what she wrote about him. I chatted with Stoppard at the memorial service for David and Jane held in October 2021.

16 x '15

Dear Adam,

Thanks for the book.

I have to say, I have avoided everything : readings, The _Mail_, God help us, + whatever else is around. But I'm sure you're having a great time, so enjoy it . What's done is done.

Best,
David

Letter from David Cornwell to me on publication of my biography of him, 16 October 2015.

suggested to me that publishing this memoir was an unhelpful act – even, perhaps, an act of sabotage. I tried not to feel that way myself, though it seemed obvious that the announcement of his book had been timed to damage mine. My suspicions were confirmed recently, when I was able to read what David had written in another private letter to Tom Stoppard, in which he designated the memoir as 'some sort of antidote to Sisman'.

This book of David's had a long history: he had been toying with the idea of writing some sort of memoir for more than half a century, in fact as long as he had been writing novels, and had made at least two previous attempts at it, in 1979 and again in 2001. In retrospect I wondered whether my book might have been the catalyst that enabled him finally to write his.

He sent me an inscribed copy of his memoir the following August, a few days before it appeared in the shops.* Inevitably he had decided to call it *The Pigeon Tunnel*, a title he had first proposed for one of his novels forty-five years earlier, and had suggested for book after book since.

Tom Weldon, chief executive of Penguin Random House, was quoted as saying that it was a 'huge honour' to publish *The Pigeon Tunnel*, which he lauded as 'the story of our times as seen through the eyes of one of this country's greatest novelists'. This

---

* My last letter from David came almost three years later, dated 16 April 2019, after I had sent him a book that I had written about a con man who in some ways resembled his father. 'I was touched that you sent me the very handsome volume of *The Professor and the Parson*, and pleased to see such glowing endorsements on the cover (and in the reviews!),' he wrote. 'I was tempted to add my own favourable thoughts, but felt it was a little creepy and might be seen as such. I think you did a lovely job with the material, and I wish the book good luck.'

was perhaps a hyperbolic description for a book consisting of thirty-eight anecdotal chapters, most of them brief (one of them only two sentences). More than half of the content (161 out of 308 pages) had been published before, though not all of the sources were acknowledged – the opening chapter, for example, 'Don't Be Beastly to Your Secret Service', had been published in the *Sunday Times* in 1986. By far the most substantial chapter was an only slightly modified version of the article 'In Ronnie's Court', published in the *New Yorker* in 2002.

The effect was episodic, and more entertaining than revealing. For John Gapper, the reviewer in the *Financial Times*, it was like listening to 'the stories, polished over time, of a British foreign correspondent in a grand hotel bar'. The same metaphor occurred to Walter Isaacson, reviewing the book in *The New York Times*:

> Reading his book is like being at the bar of Raffles with a veteran raconteur who has not expended quite enough effort determining which of his oft-told tales are profound and which a bit pointless.

David anticipated the charge that some of these stories might have become embellished in the retelling. His defence was to liken himself to his father:

> Is there really a big difference, I wonder, between the man who sits at his desk and dreams up scams on the blank page (*me*), and the man who puts on a clean shirt every morning and, with nothing in his pocket but imagination, sallies forth to con his victim (*Ronnie*)?
>
> Ronnie the conman could spin you a story out of the air, sketch in a character who did not exist, and paint a golden

opportunity where there wasn't one. He could blind you with bogus detail or helpfully clarify a non-existent knotty point if you weren't quite quick enough on the uptake to grasp the technicalities of his con first time around. He could withhold a great secret on grounds of confidentiality, then whisper it to your ear alone because he has decided to trust you.

And if all that isn't part and parcel of the writer's art, tell me what is.

The Pigeon Tunnel was subtitled 'Stories from My Life'. Its introduction contained a passing reference to my biography:

> A recently published account of my life offers thumbnail versions of one or two of the stories, so it naturally pleases me to reclaim them as my own, tell them in my own voice, and invest them as best I can with my own feelings.

There was an element of pulling rank in this statement: these are my stories, he was saying, and I can tell them best.

The same story may receive different treatment in a biography and a memoir. Memoir is what you can remember: biography aspires to objective truth, even though the biographer knows, or should know, that this is unattainable. In his introduction to *The Pigeon Tunnel* David described the contents of his memoir as 'true stories told from memory ...'

> – to which you are entitled to ask, what is truth and what is memory? ... But please be assured: Nowhere have I consciously falsified an event or a story. Disguised where necessary, yes. Falsified, emphatically not. And where my memory is shaky, I have taken care to say so.

He made no claim to factual accuracy. 'To the creative writer,' he wrote, 'fact is raw material, not his taskmaster but his instrument, and his job is to make it sing. Real truth lies, if anywhere, not in facts, but in nuance.'

This reads well enough, but what does it mean in practice? As I mentioned in the introduction to this book, while at work on my biography I found myself sometimes questioning the veracity of what I was being told, and I am afraid that the same was true while I was reading *The Pigeon Tunnel*. For example, David provides a charming account of a visit to Paris at the age of sixteen, dispatched by his father to recover money from the Panamanian ambassador, a grey-haired count. 'The door to the elegant house is opened by the most desirable woman I had ever seen,' he writes, and he describes how she comes on to the innocent schoolboy throughout the remainder of the evening, squeezing his hand, caressing his leg, and nibbling his ear, as they sip daiquiris, discuss business, and dine in a favourite Russian restaurant. Back at the house the count announces that they are ready for bed, and the countess indicates that David should join them. The schoolboy stumbles through his excuses and flees.

As told in *The Pigeon Tunnel*, this is a delightful story of innocence and naughtiness. My difficulty with it is that he had given an account of this visit before, with none of this nuance. In that version there was no suggestion of seduction; the countess was dismissed in a single phrase, and David was accompanied throughout by his older brother. So which are we to believe?

And yet maybe in raising such questions I was being a bore. As he says, these were his stories, and if he lent me a few of them for a while, he was entitled to reclaim them. It was, after all, his life.

Conclusion: truth & fiction

Much of David's behaviour described in these pages is reprehensible: dishonesty, evasion and lying, for decade after decade. Does it lower him in our estimation to know that he lied to his wife? Yes, of course it does; it is natural to feel dismay when those whom we admire behave less than well. But few individuals would be comfortable in subjecting their private behaviour to public scrutiny. I knew that I would not be myself. He that is without sin among you, let him cast the first stone.

Even the greatest writers have human flaws. David's troubled childhood helps to excuse his defects as an adult; but without that difficult childhood he would almost certainly not have become a writer.

Did the deceit detract from the quality of his work? One of the attributes that distinguishes the serious novelist is his or her ability to write about things as they are, rather than as we think they ought to be, or how we might like them to be. This takes courage, and honesty. In that sense at least, truth is important to the writer. So if David behaved discreditably, does this discredit his novels? If the writer was untrustworthy, can we trust the writing? Perhaps the answer to this conundrum lies in the distinction between the life and the work. In his finest novels, such as *A Perfect Spy*, David was unsparing of himself, confronting his demons with disarming candour. Maybe he was true to himself, if not to his wife. David Cornwell at his worst was a liar; but John le Carré at his best was a truth-teller.

And yet it is difficult not to think that the repeated deceit, and the concomitant hypocrisy, had some corrosive effect. Downstairs the man looked much the same as he had always done; but the portrait in the attic became more and more hideous.

Every great man has his disciples, wrote Oscar Wilde, and Judas is his biographer. In writing this book I have been conscious that it could be considered as an act of revenge, or even betrayal. Nobody else alive knows so much about David as I do. Is it wrong of me to reveal his secrets? As I mentioned in the introduction, David himself was relaxed about what I wrote after his death. It seems to me that one cannot fully understand or appreciate his work without at least some knowledge of his secret life; and now no one living can be harmed writing about it. Had Jane been still alive, I would have held back.

Biographers have a duty to the truth. In issues of biography as in so many aspects of life, it is worth consulting Dr Johnson. Almost three hundred years ago he challenged the prevailing orthodoxy that the biographer should conceal the failings of his subject. Respect for the dead did not mean that their faults should be suppressed or glossed over. On the contrary, 'if nothing but the bright side of characters should be shown, we should sit down in despondency, and think it utterly impossible to imitate them in *any thing*.' Finding flaws in those whom we admire can be improving, by encouraging us to believe that we can emulate those whom we admire, despite our own failings. 'If we owe regard to the memory of the dead, there is yet more respect to be paid to knowledge, to virtue, and to truth.'

*

I still find myself undecided about David Cornwell. Was he a heartless philanderer or a restless romantic? (He seems to have been both.) Is that even the right question to ask? What did love mean to him? Did he really need a muse, or was this a convenient contrivance? Trying to understand such a complicated man is like trying to find one's path through (to borrow a phrase coined in a different context) a wilderness of mirrors. Consider, for example, this passage from *A Perfect Spy*, in which Kate, a former lover of Magnus Pym, recalls how he talked about leaving his wife:

> 'I love you, Kate ... Get me clear of this and I'll marry you and we'll live happily ever after ... I'll dump Mary. We'll go and live abroad' ... Phone calls from the other end of the earth. 'I rang to say I love you.' Flowers, saying 'I love you.' Cards. Little notes folded into things, shoved under the door, personal for my eyes only in top secret envelopes. 'I've lived too long with the what-ifs. I want action, Kate. You're my escape line. Help me.'

Here David is showing us how his character Pym is lying to his mistress as well as to his wife, and perhaps also to himself. Pym is behaving just as David did, time after time. For all we know, he may have scribbled these lines while on Lesbos with Sue Dawson. And when he got home, he would have handed the pages to Jane to type. Like so much of his fiction, it is a form of confession. As so often with John le Carré, he is hiding in plain sight.

*

In a passage that David drafted for me, he asserted that none of his affairs had threatened the stability of his relationship with Jane. I think that this was probably true, at least so far as he was concerned. Jane had become indispensable to him. She possessed practical and organisational skills which helped him in his work. She was at home in the publishing world, which meant that she was able to take care of much of the necessary administration – a considerable burden, when each novel was published in thirty or more countries, in hardback and paperback, with all the attendant publicity and promotion, not to mention the subsidiary rights: film, television, radio, audiobook, and so on. Most important of all, she had an unshakeable faith in the importance of David's writing, a faith that would sustain him through periods of criticism and self-doubt.

Unlike his first wife, Jane understood that David's writing was sacred to him. It was all-important, and to it all else was subsumed. His dedication to his work was such that holidays were postponed, arrangements to see old friends cancelled, even family kept away. Writing days became too precious to squander. He had built a fortress around himself, from which he would emerge for the occasional foray, but sooner or later he would always retreat and pull up the drawbridge behind him. The resulting isolation may have been necessary for his writing, though it did not help him to see himself as others did.

David would continue working until he died, finding it hard to relax for more than a short interlude between books. For him, writing had become 'the whole of life'. While he was writing he was absorbed; and when he was not, he was edgy and uncomfortable.

*

David's philandering, which he was so desperate to conceal from the world during his lifetime, is everywhere evident in his fiction. What appear to be riddles are readily explicable when you know the truth. 'Do you know what love is?' he has one of his characters ask. 'I'll tell you: it is whatever you can still betray.'

The effect of the revelations already published, and the further revelations in this book, may be damaging to his reputation. It will no longer be possible to see John le Carré as some kind of secular saint, as some of his less critical fans were inclined to do. We live in judgemental times; and the fact that David did not always behave well in his private life may be held against him, at least for a while.

Yet in the long term I think it will be good for him for his secrets to be known. *Tout comprendre, c'est tout pardonner.* If his wife was willing to forgive his transgressions, who are we to judge him? It was not easy being David Cornwell, despite all his success. The more we can understand this complex, driven, unhappy man, the more we can appreciate his work. And in the end it is the work that survives.

Acknowledgements

Many individuals have contributed to this book in one way or another, and I am grateful to them all, even if I cannot list all their names. I owe a special debt of gratitude to Simon Cornwell, who suggested the idea for this book, though I would be the first to recognise that he has not endorsed its content and may not agree with all my judgements. Some of the ideas in this book emerged in a seminar at the University of St Andrews; and certain passages have been adapted from articles published in the *Guardian*, *Telegraph* and *Spectator*.

I wish to thank those who shared their stories with me, especially Susan Anderson, Tim Geary, Derek Johns, Verity Ravensdale, Natascha Wolf and 'Sarah'. I am also grateful to Martin Pick for allowing me to read documents from his father's archive; to Kai Bird, for information about Janet Lee Stevens; to William Shawcross, for introducing me to 'Sarah'; and to Susie Vereker for allowing me to read her correspondence with Liz Tollinton. I must thank the Harry Ransom Center, The University of Texas at Austin, for permission to publish extracts from David's letters to Susan Anderson and for use of the images reproduced on on pages 108, 110 and 118.

I am also grateful to those individuals who read and

commented on the text of this book, contributing in the process their knowledge of the subject from different perspectives: William Boyd, Alan Judd, Anthony Parker, Roland Philipps, Juliet Rice, Nicholas Shakespeare, Federico Varese, Henry Woudhuysen and Michela Wrong.

Lastly, I want to thank Andrew Franklin and his team at Profile for responding so positively to my proposal to write this book; and in particular my editor Nick Humphrey for his support, enthusiasm and encouragement.

References

DC = David Cornwell; AS = Adam Sisman

p. 1   'in an excitingly forbidden undertaking': Janet Malcolm, *The Silent Woman: Sylvia Plath and Ted Hughes* (1994), p. 9.

p. 2   'My infidelities': DC to AS, 1 February 2013.

p. 3   'It's hard not to feel': Theo Tait, 'Born to lying', *London Review of Books*, 3 December 2015 (Vol. 37, No. 23).

p. 4   *In a previous book I explored the tension*: Adam Sisman, *Boswell's Presumptuous Task* (2000).

p. 5   'A great writer requires a great biography': George Packer, 'A life split in two', *The New York Times*, 21 November 2008.
        'a laureate': Blake Morrison, 'Love and betrayal in the mist', *Times Literary Supplement*, 11 April 1986.

p. 8   'not a process that is compatible with self-knowledge': John le Carré, *The Pigeon Tunnel: Stories from My Life* (2016), pp. 8–9.

p. 9   'I couldn't possibly have shook his hand': 'Espionage is an accident' (interview with Olga Craig), *Seven* (*Sunday Telegraph* magazine), 29 August 2010.
        'dearly love': John C. Q. Roberts, *Speak Clearly into the Chandelier: Cultural Politics between Britain and Russia, 1973–2000* (2000), p. 168.

p. 18   'in relation to greater and more formative influences': DC to AS, 12 January 2015.

p. 20   *'People believe what they want to believe'*: DC to Susan Anderson, 13 July 1994.

p. 21   *a colleague who worked alongside him*: Michael Marten, *Tim Marten – Memories* (2009), p. 180.

p. 22   *'I think David was absolutely bored stiff'*: *Tim Marten – Memories*, p. 180.

p. 23   *David claimed that I had given*: Adam Sisman, *John le Carré: The Biography* (2015), p. 223 fn.

p. 25   *'women were his secret audience'*: DC, 'The enemy within', *Sunday Times*, 18 February 1968.

p. 27   *'I had time alone in those horrible little rooms'*: Nick Miller, 'John le Carré: Why I brought back Guillam, Smiley and the Cold War', *Sydney Morning Herald*, 12 September 2017.

p. 28   *'I miss the Office, always have done'*: DC to Alan Judd, 18 May 2019; Tim Cornwell (ed.), *A Private Spy: The Letters of John le Carré, 1945–2020* (2022), p. 599.

p. 29   *'John le Carré I would gladly hang, draw and quarter'*: Cited in Gordon Corera, *The Art of Betrayal: Life and Death in the British Secret Service* (2011), p. 100.

p. 30   *'There were those who were furious'*: Gordon Corera, *'Tinker Tailor Soldier Spy*: John le Carré and reality', BBC News, 11 September 2011.

p. 31   *On the contrary, David's letters to Judd*: *A Private Spy*, pp. 387–98.

p. 37   *'immense gratitude for your secret understanding of me'*: DC to Jane Cornwell, 13 March 1987; *A Private Spy*, pp. 268–9.
        David often quoted the saying: For a discussion of this point, see *A Private Spy*, pp. 304–5.

p. 38   *'I regret more than I can say'*: Letters to Tony Cornwell and to his sons, 15 May 2007 & 11 June 2001; *A Private Spy*, pp. 482–4 & 455–6.

p. 39   *'I was a caged animal'*: DC to AS, 24 April 2014.

p. 40   *'very tall, big-eyed, and radiant'*: DC to Ines Schlenker, 15 September 2004; Motesiczky archive, Tate Gallery.

p. 41   '*I am going away to write a book*': DC to Ann Cornwell, 28 May 1968.

      He listed the 'Reasons' for his philandering: DC to AS, 1 February 2013.

p. 47   '*a terrible problem, about friendship*': DC to Susan Anderson, 19 March 1994.

p. 57   '*From early on in our marriage*': DC to AS, 1 February 2013.

p. 58   '*So many men fantasize*': DC to Olive Hill, 8 September 1988; *A Private Spy*, pp. 288–90.

p. 66   '*I see him at the house of his friend*': Undated letter containing a draft of Yvette Pierpaoli's book *Femme aux milles enfants* (1992).

p. 67   '*I've known him now for nearly twenty years*': Translated extract from *Femme aux milles enfants*.

p. 78   '*there is no compromise*': DC to Verity Ravensdale, 25 October 1982.

p. 80   *Though there is no evidence for this*: Kai Bird, *The Good Spy: The Life and Death of Robert Ames* (2014); *A Private Spy*, pp. 253–4.

p. 127   '*Do you mind as much as I do*': Liz Tollinton to Susan Vereker (Kennaway), 28 March 1983.

p. 128   *a biography of James Kennaway*: Trevor Royle, *James and Jim: A Biography of James Kennaway* (1983).

      '*I felt rather sad somehow*': Liz Tollinton to Susan Vereker (Kennaway), 8 September 1983.

      '*How David would have hated to know*'; '*they are far too revealing*'; '*He seems to see-saw*': Liz Tollinton to Charles Pick, 24 April 1992, 17 August 1992 & 4 February 1993.

p. 136   '*I had an amazing life*'; '*You gave me my life*': DC to his sons and Jane, 11 June 2001; DC to Jane Cornwell, 21 February 2003 & 13 March 1987; *A Private Spy*, pp. 455–7, 467 & 268–9.

p. 137   '*I have no idea of course*': DC to Verity Ravensdale, 1 March 2006.

p. 138   '*It's very hard for me*'; '*Who is writing what when?*': DC to Verity Ravensdale, 13 & 25 March 2006.

p. 141 '*One Adam Sisman*': DC to Sir John Margetson, 3 August 2011; *A Private Spy*, pp. 517–18.

'*I have put my trust in him*': DC to Susan Vereker, 21 January 2011.

'*is emphatically not an authorised one*': DC to Martin Pick, 19 November 2011.

p. 146 '*Wherever you've been*': DC to AS, 21 January 2012.

'*to have an "Inspector Calls" in one's life*': DC to Tony Cornwell, 4 February 2012; *A Private Spy*, pp. 524–6.

p. 147 '*I have never disguised from you*': DC to AS, 26 December 2012.

p. 148 '*As you may imagine*', '*It is no coincidence that in "Spy"*': DC to AS, 1 February 2013.

p. 149 '*I need a bit of space & time*': DC to AS, 4 February 2013.

p. 150 '*We know you hope to publish*': Jane Cornwell to AS, 15 December 2013.

p. 151 '*It felt to me then as though we were two characters*': Suleika Dawson, *The Secret Heart* (2022), p. 228.

'*I trust you, & I think you trust me*': DC to AS, 16 March 2014.

p. 154 '*Your book might profit by telling people*': DC to AS, 7 April 2014.

'*Your book as it stands is not doing its job*': DC to AS, 24 April 2014.

p. 155 '*I cannot continue to help you with your book*': DC to AS, 2 January 2015.

p. 159 '*I am, always shall be, like most people of my generation, wary of Germany*': DC to AS, 12 January 2015.

p. 161 '*me grappling feebly with the moral issues*': Ian Hamilton, *In Search of J. D. Salinger* (1988), p. 9.

'*If you are able to accept the changes as they stand*': DC to AS, 4 February 2015.

p. 162 '*There will be many other points*': DC to AS, 4 February 2015.

Sometimes the discussion was circular: AS to DC, 19 May 2015.

p. 163 '*I'm sure you're having a great time*': DC to AS, 16 October 2015.

p. 165 *'some sort of antidote to Sisman'*: DC to Sir Tom Stoppard, 1 June 2015; *A Private Spy*, pp. 550–51.

p. 166 *'the stories, polished over time'*: John Gapper, '*The Pigeon Tunnel* by John le Carré – a delicate truth', *Financial Times*, 6 September 2016.

'Reading his book is like being at the bar': Walter Isaacson, 'John le Carré's memoir about his journey from spy to novelist', *The New York Times*, 13 September 2016.

'Is there really a big difference, I wonder': *The Pigeon Tunnel*, pp. 282–3.

p. 168 *he had given an account of this visit before*: 'In Ronnie's court', *New Yorker*, 18 February 2002.

Index

Page numbers in *italics* indicate illustrations; *n* indicates a footnote